92
CHA
   Gonzales, Doreen
     Cesar Chavez: leader
   for migrant workers

DATE DUE			
FEB 1 8 2000			
12/13			

CESAR CHAVEZ

Leader for Migrant Farm Workers

Doreen Gonzales

Winters High School
101 Grant Avenue
Winters, CA 95694

ENSLOW PUBLISHERS, INC.

44 Fadem Road
Box 699
Springfield, N.J. 07081
U.S.A.

P.O. Box 38
Aldershot
Hants GU12 6BP
U.K.

Library of Congress Cataloging-in-Publication Data

Gonzales, Doreen.
    Cesar Chavez : leader for migrant farm workers / Doreen Gonzales.
        p. cm. — (Hispanic biographies)
    Includes bibliographical references and index.
    Summary: Examines the life of the Mexican American labor organizer who demanded rights for migrant farm workers.
    ISBN 0-89490-760-3
    1. Chavez, Cesar, 1927–1993 —Juvenile literature. 2. Labor leaders—United States—Biography—Juvenile literature. 3. Trade-unions—Migrant agricultural laborers—United States—Officials and employees—Biography—Juvenile literature. 4. Mexican Americans—Biography—Juvenile literature. 5. United Farm Workers—History—Juvenile literature. [1. Chavez, Cesar, 1927–1993. 2. Labor leaders. 3. Mexican Americans—Biography. 4. United Farm Workers—History.] I. Title. II. Series.
HD6509.C48G65 1996
331.88'13'092—dc20
[B]   95-34696
                                                         CIP
                                                          AC

Printed in the United States of America

10 9 8 7 6 5 4 3

Illustration Credits: Victor Aleman, photographer, Cesar E. Chavez Foundation, P.O. Box 62, Keene, Calif., 93531, p. 112; Jocelyn Sherman, Cesar E. Chavez Foundation, p. 114; Cesar E. Chavez Foundation, pp. 27, 47, 117; Archives of Labor and Union Affairs, Wayne State University, pp. 8, 23, 30, 38, 43, 60, 63, 71, 77, 91, 95, 98; Cesar E. Chavez Foundation and Archives of Labor and Union Affairs, Wayne State University, pp. 19, 84.

Cover Illustration: Victor Aleman, photographer, Cesar E. Chavez Foundation

CONTENTS

CHAPTER ONE

TOIL AND INDIGNITY

 Although he was only sixteen, Cesar Chavez did the work of a man. Many days he labored from dawn until dusk. The job he hated most was cutting broccoli. Slipping and sliding through wet, muddy fields, Cesar was thoroughly soaked long before his workday ended. Without proper clothing, his hands and feet stayed icy for hours in the January cold. Though each of Cesar's days was a grueling repetition of the one before, he always worked. His parents depended on him to help buy food for his brothers and sisters.

Cesar was a migrant farm worker who had sown, tended, and picked countless crops. At sixteen, he had already mastered a variety of farm jobs. He had planted crops by hand, sometimes in soil so thorny it punctured his fingers over and over again. "It hurt," he later said, "but [I] couldn't stop. We had to make that acre."[1] He had thinned and weeded plants, walking row upon row in a twisted, hunched over position that left his youthful body a bundle of aches. And he had harvested crops, at times pulling fifteen-pound sugar beets from soil so stubborn his hands split open. Yet for all of this painful labor, Cesar was still poor. On one job he was paid only twelve cents an hour. At another he earned just fifty cents for filling an entire bushel basket with lima beans.

Unfortunately, Cesar was not unique. He was one of thousands of migrant farm laborers who tended the fertile fields of California's valleys. The days were long and hard for these workers. According to one writer, the men and women who picked America's food were no better off than slaves. Statistics backed this up. In 1965, the best-paid migrant farm workers earned only $1.50 an hour, and a family's annual income was frequently equal to less than one-half the poverty level.[2] Therefore, most field workers could not adequately feed or clothe themselves. Three well-balanced meals a day were a luxury few knew, and hundreds lunched on nothing more than a potato sandwich or a tortilla. Proper clothing was a luxury, too, and shoes were an especially coveted commodity. As one sixteen-year-old migrant reported, "We only wear shoes in the summer when we go to church. They are expensive, and we must make them last."[3]

Decent homes were also unaffordable. Some farmers provided housing for migrant laborers, but its quality varied from farm to farm. Too often the housing was no more than a converted chicken coop or storage shed where dozens of families shared one outhouse and an outdoor faucet. After the secretary of Labor toured one camp in the 1960s he remarked, "I'm glad I hadn't eaten first. I would have vomited."[4] Some migrants lived outside the camps in plywood shanties that seldom had heating or plumbing. Others slept in cars, or under bridges, or they built crude shelters of cardboard to call home. For many the only source of drinking and bathing water was a nearby irrigation ditch.

Though some farm owners showed concern for their seasonal employees, others exploited them to increase their own profits. The harder and longer the migrants worked the more money a farmer could make. Therefore, most laborers were in the

M any migrant workers in the late 1960s lived in labor camps owned by their employers. These migrant children's home is typical of the kind found in those camps.

fields by 6:00 A.M. and they worked for ten or twelve hours. The jobs they performed were physically demanding. For example, a number of tasks required walking bent at the waist. This was tortuous when done for several hours at a time, and it was not unusual for workers to go directly from the fields to bed until the next morning. Even jobs that could be done upright required stamina, and workers weren't given sufficient rest breaks. These punishing days were one reason why so many migrant workers died before they turned fifty years of age.[5]

Yet, few farmers provided seasonal employees with basic necessities. Rarely was drinking water available, and field temperatures frequently exceeded one hundred degrees. Farmers who did provide water often supplied a single cup to be shared by all. Toilets, too, were absent, forcing workers to search for private areas in which to relieve themselves. Not only was this an issue of personal dignity, but it was also a health issue. People who are not provided with toilet facilities suffer from an abnormally high rate of parasitic diseases. Women, especially, have an increased number of bladder illnesses when there are no toilets in the fields.

Farmers exhibited further lack of concern for their employees' health by failing to make the work environment safe. Field laborers were frequently injured in serious, but preventable accidents. Worse still, some farmers showed no sympathy for employees hurt on the job. Rosa Castillo's husband, for example, was injured while moving heavy sacks of fertilizer on an old platform. When the floor beneath him gave way Mr. Castillo fell through, and the accident left him bedridden for six months. While he was recovering the Castillos were forced to move, because the farmer didn't want a family in his camp if every member of that family wasn't working.[6]

This was not an unusual requirement, but it was hardly necessary. It was a matter of survival for migrants to employ each able-bodied family member. Having both parents in the fields, however, presented another problem. Families with small children often had no one to care for the youngsters while they worked. This forced parents to take children into the hot, insect-ridden fields. Unhealthy at best, this practice sometimes proved fatal. Such was the case for the Chapa family when their four-year-old son was run over by a potato-digging machine in 1965.[7]

An inadequate diet, unsanitary housing, and arduous working conditions resulted in migrants having the highest rate of disease and death amongst any group of American workers. Saddest of all, migrant children had little chance of escaping this way of life. Because families moved as crops in various places needed tending, children were constantly transferred from school to school. Rarely did a child become established in one before it was time to move on. Migrant children typically attended several different schools each year. This meant their education was a "hit or miss" process, and the constant interruptions caused even the brightest children to fall behind. The average child received up to only a fourth-grade education.[8]

To make matters worse, schools treated migrant children with less respect than the children who lived in an area all year long. Administrators, teachers, parents, and permanent students looked down upon seasonal workers. Cesar's experience was evidence of this. When he was in school, he was given battered books and pencil stubs considered not good enough for the other students. This kind of treatment humiliated Cesar, as it must have thousands of migrant children. Additional embarrassment came from being mocked because of inadequate clothing. Consequently, school was a hostile place for the children of farm workers, even though a good education would break their cycle of poverty.

Those children who were not driven from

school had their education cut short due to financial need. Many dropped out as soon as they were old enough to work; for some, this was as young as eight or nine years of age. Most migrant children ended their education before they were teenagers. Youngsters either worked in the fields or cared for siblings while their mothers worked. A 1957 law prohibited children younger than sixteen from working during school hours, but some farmers ignored it. One inspection found children illegally employed on 60 percent of the farms studied.[9]

But how could such a dismal cycle of poverty exist in America, the land of opportunity? Seasonal labor has always been an important part of the nation's farm economy. Even today, temporary laborers work in farm fields all across the country. According to the U.S. Department of Labor, about 55 percent of these seasonal workers are United States citizens or permanent residents. Thirty-three percent are citizens of another country who have been authorized to work in the United States. The remaining 12 percent are not citizens of the United States and are working here without permission. The people who work as seasonal agricultural laborers maintain much the same migratory patterns they did in the 1940s when Cesar's family worked in the fields.[10]

Each spring, thousands of migrants spread out across the country to cultivate and harvest the crops that fed the nation. Some of these seasonal workers were single men and women or fathers working away from home. But a large portion of migrants traveled as families, with every able member working in the field. Beginning in warm southern states, farm workers followed spring as it crept northward. Large numbers moved up the Eastern seaboard and across the Midwest. Many, such as Cesar's family, began in the Southwest and worked their way north through the valleys of California.

Several California farms were not small operations, but huge ranches that covered thousands of acres. Owned by individuals or corporations, these ranches were really food factories which employed hundreds of workers. The owners were called growers, and their ranches were referred to as agribusinesses. Agribusiness owners were interested in the same thing all businesspeople are interested in—profits. To maintain the highest profits possible, growers wanted to keep their costs down. One way to do this was by paying their labor low wages.

This practice had been established early in California history. Native Americans were the first group to be exploited. They were forced to work for the Spanish settlers who appeared in the area during the early 1800s. At the time, Spain claimed all of California and much of what is now considered the American Southwest. Soon after Mexico won its independence from Spain in 1821, this land became a part of Mexico. Large numbers of American settlers entered the area during the 1840s, hungry for land of their own. To satisfy this hunger the United States declared war on Mexico in 1846, demanding that Mexico surrender its northern lands. In 1848, a defeated Mexican government did just that, giving nearly half its total land to the United States. Suddenly, the eighty thousand Mexicans living on this land became American citizens. The original peace agreement between Mexico and the United States assured these Mexican Americans that they could keep the land they owned. But many lost their land to white settlers in lengthy and costly court proceedings. With no other means of survival, they became the poorly paid employees on other people's farms.

During the 1860s, Chinese people immigrated to California to work on the first transcontinental railroad. Once the tracks were laid, they too turned to farm work. Next came large numbers of Japanese immigrants. When a bloody revolution broke out in Mexico in 1910, Mexicans began leaving their country by the hundreds of thousands. Eager to avoid the turmoil in Mexico, the Mexicans were willing to work for low wages. Most settled in the Southwest, and once again, California ranchers were provided with cheap labor.

The 1920s brought Filipino immigrants to California fields. They were followed by the poverty-stricken farmers which the Great Depression and drought of the 1930s had left homeless. When World War II created a shortage of farm laborers, Mexican field hands were brought across the border by the busload. Many stayed. By 1964, migrant workers were of varied backgrounds—Native-American, Asian, white, African-American, and Mexican. By far though, Mexicans made up the largest group.[11]

Regardless of their ethnic background, migrant laborers were the most poorly paid, fed, housed, and educated workers in America. This was partially because there were no laws to protect them. In 1935, the United States government had passed the National Labor Relations Act (NLRA). This law stated that all workers must be paid a minimum wage and could not be forced to work long hours each day. The NLRA also forced employers to allow their workers to form unions. A union is a group of employees who join together to improve their working conditions. Unions choose representatives who talk directly with an employer on behalf of all the members. These representatives negotiate the wages and benefits workers will receive. They also help workers settle complaints with employers.

Although business owners sometimes have to pay higher wages when their workers form a union, they can benefit from having their businesses unionized. Because union members tend to be loyal to an organization that is concerned with their welfare, they are more likely to resolve a problem than to simply quit their jobs. Therefore, employers with unionized workers maintain a stable work force. This is often less costly than hiring cheap labor with a high rate of turnover.

Still, some employers did not want unions in their businesses. They were afraid they would lose too much control over their labor. To keep them out, they fired or intimidated employees they suspected of organizing a union. But the NLRA said this could no longer be done. It ordered employers to accept unions if their workers wanted one. This is called "recognizing a union." After the NLRA was enacted, all employers had to recognize unions if their workers voted for one. All employers, that is, except farmers.

Unfortunately, the NLRA specifically excluded farm workers from the labor laws. This gave individual growers the right to make their own rules. Growers could set their own wages. They could require migrant laborers to work twelve-hour days and could fire them at any time for no reason. Perhaps most significantly, growers did not have to recognize unions.

Even so, farm workers tried to organize to improve their working conditions. One common tactic of the workers was to "strike" a farm. During a strike, employees refuse to work and a business owner is left without a labor force. It is difficult, however, for poor people to strike. Many have no money saved, and they face hunger when they don't work. Still, throughout the early 1900s, a few farm strikes attracted large numbers of workers. The growers quickly responded. Sometimes they brought in laborers from other regions to work their fields. Often, strike organizers were beaten and jailed. Some were even killed. Violence and terrorism were the tools that growers favored to discourage farm workers from creating unions. Frequently, law enforcement agencies supported the growers. Without the help of the NLRA, farm workers had no laws to back up their efforts. Therefore, they remained without a union to represent them.

There seemed to be very little hope for

change—until Cesar Chavez. As an adult, Chavez decided that the gatherers of America's food deserved better. He found it absurd that California guaranteed liquor manufacturers a minimum price for liquor but didn't guarantee farm workers a living wage. He was not alone. After interviewing migrant families in 1969, writer Sandra Weiner was also overcome by the irony of the situation. Here were people raising the nation's food "under the open sky on the rich earth . . . harvesting nature's bounty."[12] Yet their lives were miserable, and they were given nothing in return except, as Weiner said, "the endless toil of picking a ton of fruit."[13]

Having picked more than a ton of fruit himself, Chavez intimately understood the farm workers' dilemma. Through determination, sacrifice, and creativity, he alerted America to their impoverished lives. More importantly, he demanded change. In time, Chavez commanded the first effective union of farm workers in the country. This in itself was close to a miracle.

But Chavez did more. As a Mexican American, he proclaimed pride in his Mexican heritage. By encouraging others to do the same, he sparked self-respect in Hispanic people all over the country. Regardless of class or age, they became inspired to light the ethnic fire inside themselves. Yet Chavez's significance went deeper still. In giving

Cesar Chavez organized field laborers into a union that fought for better working and living conditions.

dignity to the farm workers, he gave all poor people pride despite their poverty. For them, he represented humanity and equality. At the time of his death, Cesar Chavez was famous the world round. For thousands of people he symbolized the right of every person to lead a decent life regardless of color, occupation, or economic status. The story of Cesar Chavez is one of struggle and love; it is the story of an American hero.

UPROOTED

 During the late 1880s, huge ranches that required large labor forces covered northern Mexico. The people who worked on these ranches were paid low wages and lived in tiny shacks on the ranches. The wealthy ranch owners fed and clothed their employees, but treated them like slaves. When a baby was born to an employee, the rancher began charging the child for food, clothing, and shelter. By the time the child was old enough to work, he or she was deep in debt to the rancher. For most there was no way to repay this debt except by working on the ranch.

Each year a little of an employee's debt was paid, but more debt for that year accumulated. The ranch owners arranged this system so that none of their workers was ever able to pay off his debt and leave the ranch. In this way, the landowners maintained a sufficient supply of cheap labor for running their operations.

Cesario Chavez (Cesar's grandfather) worked on one such ranch called the Hacienda del Carmen. When a worker on the hacienda (ranch) rebelled or complained, he was promptly sent off to serve in the Mexican army. Chavez was a man who could not keep quiet in the face of injustice. He frequently spoke out when he saw someone treated unfairly. Because of his outspokenness, the owner decided to send Chavez to the army. But when Chavez learned of the owner's plan, he ran away, leaving behind his wife and children. Chavez escaped into the night and crossed the Rio Grande River near El Paso, Texas.

In the United States, Chavez found a job with a railroad. Sometimes he worked on farms. Always he saved his money until he had enough to bring his family to the United States. When Mrs. Chavez crossed the border in 1888, she brought along fourteen children, including two-year-old Librado.

The Chavezes settled in Arizona three years before it became a state. In the North Gila Valley near Yuma, the family claimed over one hundred acres of land to homestead.[1] There they built an adobe house divided in half by a covered breezeway. Two-foot-thick mud walls kept the family warm in the winter and cool in the summer. With shovels and sweat, the Chavez men dug irrigation ditches to divert water from the Colorado River across their land. Without the water, no crops would grow. In time, their labor coaxed corn, squash, chili peppers, and watermelon from the desert soil, and the farm fed the family.

As the Chavez children grew and married, they moved from the house to build farms of their own. One of the last to leave was Librado. He married Juana Estrada in 1924, and their first child, Rita, was born in 1925. Soon the couple bought a nearby grocery store with an adjoining gas station and tiny pool hall. They lived in an apartment above the store. Librado was a hard worker and continued to work the farm, too.

On March 31, 1927, Cesario Estrada Chavez was born, a boy named for his grandfather and mother. He had the dark skin and hair of a native Mexican, and it would not be long before there was a mischievous twinkle in his dark eyes. In time, Cesario would be known as Cesar.

Two years after Cesario's birth, the United States plunged into the Great Depression. This

When Chavez returned to his Gila Valley home in 1969, parts of it were still standing. This photograph clearly shows the two wings of the adobe house where three generations of Chavezes lived.

was a time when many Americans lost their jobs and homes, and farmers were paid low prices for their crops—if they were able to sell them at all. Most of the farmers who lived in the Gila Valley barely made ends meet before the Depression. Now they were even poorer. But Librado was kind and generous and let destitute people buy food at his store on credit. His customers had children to feed, and Librado could not deny them food. Few, though, were ever able to repay Librado, and he eventually fell into debt. This, in addition to other problems, forced Librado to sell his business. In 1932, the Chavezes moved their four children back to Librado's childhood adobe home. Little Cesario was five. He would soon have two more siblings.

Cesario's new home seemed huge. His grandfather was now dead, and his grandmother occupied the south wing of the house with his aunt. Cesario's family lived in the north wing, which was really one large room. Two small windows dimly lit the well-worn wooden floor. The sixteen by thirty-two foot area was furnished with three beds, a table, a wood-burning stove, an icebox, and a pool table Librado had brought from the pool hall. Not liking their beds, Cesario and his younger brother, Richard, preferred sleeping on top of the pool table each night. As they drifted off to sleep, the boys liked imagining they saw various shapes in the places where plaster had chipped from the walls.

Outside was a small yard with trees where Cesario and his siblings played. Mesquite bushes bordered the area. There was no electricity or running water on the Chavez farm, but just beyond the door, an irrigation canal brought water to the family. The water, tinted red from the soil, was stored in fifty-gallon barrels until the dirt settled to the bottom. Then it could be used for cooking and drinking. Across the canal were corrals where the Chavezes kept their horses.

Cesario's early years were happy. He was surrounded by a large, loving family and his life revolved around them. His parents were patient and understanding, even when Cesario and Richard played tricks on their elderly grandmother. Mrs. Chavez hugged and kissed her children frequently, and Cesario's father was affectionate, too. Librado played with the children when he could, showing them how to fashion toy cars from old sardine cans. But there was little free time on the Chavez farm. As soon as he was able, young Cesario worked. He rose early each morning to get the day's water, feed the livestock, and gather eggs. Then he would get ready for school. This included putting on shoes, which Cesario didn't like.

In fact, there wasn't much about school Cesario did like. The wooden building was a mile down the valley, and this was an especially difficult journey in the winter since the Chavez children had no warm clothing. On cold days, the long walk to school was miserable. With aunts and uncles who lived all along the way, the children scampered from one home to the next trying to keep warm.

Most of the youngsters at the Gila Valley

school were much like the Chavez children. Of Mexican descent, they had grown up speaking Spanish in their homes. The teachers, however, spoke English and insisted that the students speak English, too. Some teachers told students that if they wanted to speak Spanish, they should go back to Mexico. Children who spoke Spanish were promptly punished. As an adult, Cesar could clearly recall being disciplined for this with a ruler that "[whistled] through the air as its edge came down sharply across my knuckles."[2] The principal even spanked children with a board when they spoke Spanish. Cesario deeply resented this.

But the physical punishments weren't Cesario's greatest hurts. Worse was the humiliation he endured for mispronouncing an English word or making a mistake in grammar. Cesario felt belittled by his teachers' rejection of his language and heritage. When he called himself Mexican, a teacher would tell him, "Oh, no, don't say that!"[3] One teacher took the liberty of changing Cesario's name to something that sounded less Mexican to her—"Cesar."[4] This was the name he would be known by for the rest of his life.

The only thing Cesar liked about school was the bell that signalled the end of the day. When it rang, he leapt from his seat, took off his shoes, and began running. Often he stopped by his

A young, barefooted Cesar and his sister, Rita, pose for a photograph near their Gila Valley home.

relatives on the way home to say hello. Although they were all poor, they always had something to give Cesar, even if it was only a glass of water. Everyone stopped working to talk with him.

Perhaps Cesar's most important education came from his family. His short, slender mother was deeply religious. She followed the Catholic faith. She was a talkative woman who taught her children with *dichos* which are Mexican proverbs. For instance, she frequently told the Chavez children that "What you do to others, others do to you," and "He who holds the cow, sins as much as he who kills her."

In addition to the dichos, Mrs. Chavez told stories which taught lessons. Her tales were about honesty and obedience. Some illustrated the virtues of nonviolence. When the Chavez children argued, she would say, "It takes two to fight, and one can't do it alone."[5] Because Mrs. Chavez believed in the teachings of the Bible, she taught her children to "turn the other cheek."

Mrs. Chavez also believed it was her Christian duty to help the poor. She often invited homeless or hungry people to the Chavez house for a meal. Many times she would go searching for someone in need. When she couldn't go herself, she sent Cesar and Richard out with instructions to bring a needy person home for supper.

The people she fed usually offered to work

around the farm to repay her. But Mrs. Chavez always refused their help, reasoning that if she accepted, her food wouldn't be a gift. This selfless giving made a lasting impression on Cesar who would one day offer his own gifts to those in need.

Though there were no churches in the valley, Cesar received formal religious instruction from his grandmother. She had grown up in a Catholic convent and had a thorough understanding of the religion. But she was very old and in poor health, so she spent most of her time in bed praying. Each evening the Chavez children gathered in front of her bed to pray. During long prayers, they would grow restless. But if they giggled, Cesar's grandmother would hit them with her cane. After the prayers came Grandmother Chavez's lessons about Catholicism. From her, Cesar learned about the beliefs, customs, and saints of the Catholic religion.

When Cesar was seven or eight years old, he and his sister, Rita, were taken to the Catholic church in Yuma to receive their first communion. The priest there initially refused to accept them, saying they must have a firm understanding of the Catholic faith. But Mrs. Chavez suggested he test the two, so he drilled the children with questions about Catholicism. Cesar and Rita had been good learners, and the priest was impressed. Dressed in new clothes, the youngsters took their first

This photograph of the Gila Valley school Cesar attended was taken in 1971.

communion the next day. Along with his mother's informal religious teachings, Cesar's early formal training guided him the rest of his life.

Although they were poor, the Chavez family always had plenty of vegetables, eggs, and milk on the table. For meat, there seemed to be an endless supply of chickens. Cesar remembered having only to look under a tree or a bush to find one. The Chavez farm, in fact, was so productive the family had surplus to sell to others. But people could not always pay the Chavezes with cash, partially because of the poverty brought on by the Depression. The situation worsened when a drought spread across the Midwest and into the Southwest, beginning around 1933. River waters receded and irrigation ditches which had once been full slowed to a trickle. With little water, many crops wilted under the hot Southwestern sun.

For a long time, thousands of farm families lived in severe poverty. So they bartered. Regularly, the Chavez family traded eggs for flour or bread. This, in turn, left them without cash, so they too traded, to get by. They once paid a doctor in watermelon. But there was one expense for which the family couldn't barter—the taxes which had to be paid on the land.

To help the family, Cesar and Richard trapped gophers, earning one cent from the government for each one they killed. Gophers often tunneled through the ground and undermined the walls of irrigation canals throughout the valley. A penny per gopher, however, didn't go far. Every year, the family could not pay its land taxes and fell deeper in debt. By the time the taxes were finally due in 1937, the Chavezes' bill totaled over four thousand dollars.[6]

The federal government brought some relief to the area when it built a dam near Yuma in 1936. This project created jobs to bring money back into the valley. By renting out the pool hall and gas station he had once owned, Librado earned much-needed cash. Now after school, Cesar and Richard went straight to the station to pump gas. When they could, they played pool, becoming excellent players.

Summers brought change in the rhythm of Cesar's life. Every morning during the warm months, the family rose at 4:00 A.M. to do farm work before the intense heat made outdoor tasks impossible. As the sun set, aunts, uncles, and cousins gathered at the Chavez farm to cook their supper in a barbecue pit, picnicking on watermelon and roasted corn. When it grew dark, the children went to their beds which had been moved outside for the summer. As the grown-ups talked into the night, the children listened.

Sometimes the adults talked about relatives who had died before the children were born. Other times they told stories from the Bible. But Cesar also heard numerous accounts of the injustices poor people in Mexico had suffered. From these tales, Cesar learned how cruelly some wealthy landowners had treated their employees, and how these people had feared for their safety and their lives. Cesar also heard about the battles poor Mexicans had waged to fight for their rights. He heard about the Mexican Revolution in which the downtrodden risked their lives fighting for equality and land. From these stories Cesar deduced that it was honorable to stand up for one's rights. This idea was reinforced by Librado when the taxes on the Chavez land finally came due.

In 1937, the grace period for the Chavezes' tax payment ran out. Because the family didn't have enough money to pay their bill, the state took possession of the farm. Yet, Librado refused to let go of the land his family had owned and worked for almost thirty years. He visited banks and asked for loans. He talked to lawyers and made a desperate appeal to the governor in Phoenix. No one helped.

Still, as the months passed, Librado clung to the hope that he might be able to hold on to the land. In 1938, he went to California looking for work. The family followed and stayed through the harvest.[7] With their meager earnings, the Chavezes returned to the Gila Valley in an attempt to regain the land. In 1939, however, their homestead was sold at a public auction to a wealthy landowner in the area. Librado did not have enough money to buy it back.[8]

Soon a loud rumbling tractor rolled onto the land to tear the farm apart. Trees, which had grown up with the Chavez children and shaded them in their play, were pulled up by their roots.

Ditches, which three generations of Chavez men had carefully tended, were demolished. And, like Lincoln Logs being knocked down by a child's toy tractor, the livestock corrals were destroyed.

In helpless horror, Cesar and his family watched the destruction. Then, with no other choice, they packed their belongings into the car. Crammed with clothes, bedding, and people, the automobile turned away from the Gila Valley. Like thousands of other Americans who had lost their farms in the Depression and the drought, the Chavezes headed toward California in search of a new life.

FOLLOWING THE CROPS

Hundreds of thousands of unemployed farm workers migrated to California in the 1930s, lured by rumors of work on huge farms. Like the Chavezes, they hoped to find jobs that would put food on their tables and clothes on their backs. The Chavezes also harbored the hope of someday buying back their Gila Valley land.

It would take only a few months before the harsh realities of migratory labor shattered that dream. Much like the wealthy ranch owners Cesar's grandfather had escaped in Mexico, many California growers became rich by hiring workers at low wages. The arrival of poor people during the Depression provided growers with a ready source of cheap labor. Some landowners took advantage of the thousands desperate to find work by hiring "recruiters." Recruiters were paid according to the number of people they sent to a particular farm, regardless of whether or not the farm had enough jobs for them all. The more people who showed up at a farm, the lower the wages that grower could pay.

To entice migrants to their farms, recruiters often lied about the working conditions there, telling families that the wages were high or the housing especially good. Hearing this, hundreds of people flocked to the farm, arriving to find hordes of others competing for the same jobs. They also found the working conditions worse than recruiters had described. Wages were lower than those promised, and "good housing" often meant a tiny shack with a dirt floor and no heat, electricity, or running water. Unfortunately, most families were so poor they couldn't pass up any work they were offered. If they did, there was always someone behind them waiting to take the job.

At first, the Chavez family was trusting and knew nothing about unscrupulous recruiters. Arriving in California, they drove to Atascadero, having heard of work there. By the time they reached the fields, the harvesting had already ended. When someone told them of work in Gonzales, they traveled the one hundred miles north to find people everywhere—but no jobs.

The next recruiter sent them to Half Moon Bay where the wages turned out to be a fraction of what they had been told. But there was work, and so the Chavezes picked peas, one of several jobs referred to as "stoop labor." Walking rows of peas while bent at the waist was painful and exhausting work. The Chavez family spent two hours filling a hamper with peas, but when they carried it to the end of the field for weighing, they were told the grower only wanted "good peas." After the supervisor sorted them, Cesar and his family returned to the field to finish filling the hamper. In all the job took three hours, and the entire family earned only twenty cents.

Next the Chavezes drove to San Jose to pick cherries. There, unfortunately, the story was a familiar one. As hundreds of other migrant laborers converged on the area, growers were able to pay low wages. And, of course, there was no proper housing. In San Jose, poor Mexican Americans lived in a neighborhood of tiny homes clustered up and down two unpaved streets. The makeshift houses were crammed together with outdoor toilets in the back. A poor neighborhood

These workers are pulling weeds under the watchful eyes of supervisors. "Stoop labor" such as this is painful, but common for field laborers.

of mostly Hispanic people is sometimes called a *barrio*. Appropriately enough, this barrio was nicknamed *Sal Si Puedes,* Spanish for "get out if you can." Cesar later joked that the Chavezes first problem in Sal Si Puedes wasn't getting out, it was getting in. Because of the overcrowding, they could find nothing more than one room in a lodging house for the eleven family members traveling with them.

In San Jose, the Chavezes picked cherries, apricots, and prunes. Although everyone helped, they rarely earned more than thirty cents a day. Next, the family drove to Oxnard where they harvested walnuts. Picking walnuts was hard work, and Librado was the only one strong enough to shake the nuts loose from the trees. After jolting the walnuts free, he rested while the others gathered them from the ground.

By now it was late fall. Cesar would remember the coming winter as one of the worst in his life. When the walnuts were harvested, there was no more work. And though the Chavezes had bought little more than food and housing throughout the summer and fall, they still had no money and no place to live. Fortunately, one kind woman let the family stay in a tent in her yard. It was a small tent, and Cesar and his brothers had to sleep outside. The winter was cold and wet, and the family had little to eat. Their only food was the fish they could catch and the wild mustard greens they collected. It seemed to Cesar that he was always hungry and never warm.

The damp air presented Cesar with another

problem—that of finding a dry spot for his shoes at night. Though he tried putting them in different places, he was never successful at keeping them dry, and they soon rotted. This forced Cesar to go to school barefoot, and the other children teased him mercilessly. One thing hadn't changed since leaving Gila Valley—Cesar still hated school.

During the course of the next several years, the family would be traveling constantly, and the Chavez children would not attend any school for longer than a few months. Cesar once counted more than three dozen elementary schools he had attended.[1] None was pleasant, but he much preferred the schools populated by migrant children only. At these schools, he felt comfortable amongst the other students. But in schools where farm workers' children were a minority, Cesar felt out of place and scorned. At these schools he wasn't allowed to speak Spanish, and he was stung by racism.

Unfortunately, discrimination also existed outside the school. Memories of racism during his childhood years haunted Cesar the rest of his life. He long remembered the humiliation he felt when realizing the "No Dogs or Mexicans Allowed" signs on businesses were referring to him. He never forgot his father's look of hurt and shock at being ordered from a coffee shop because he was

Mexican-American. Once Cesar ran in tears from a "whites only" hamburger stand while a waitress laughed and called him a "dumb Mex." As an adult, Cesar said, "That laugh rang in my ears for twenty years—it seemed to cut us out of the human race."[2] Tired of such treatment, Cesar once spoke out to the owner of a diner. "Why do you have to treat people like that?" he asked. "A man who behaves like you do is not even a human being!"[3]

But Cesar was still too young to do much about racism. He was also too busy. When he wasn't at school or working next to his parents in the fields, he was earning money in other ways. During his childhood, Cesar held a variety of odd jobs, including shelling walnuts, chopping wood, shining shoes, and selling newspapers. Some Sundays, Cesar and Richard worked as a team at churches where people customarily threw coins to children after baptism ceremonies. Cesar blocked the other youngsters while Richard grabbed the money. For a while, Cesar and Richard cleaned a movie theater every day after school for a weekly salary of a nickel and a free pass to a show. The movie passes were the only "wages" Cesar ever kept for himself. All of his other earnings went to his parents, and Cesar was proud he could help the family. By the time he was twelve years old, Cesar was working after school every day and ten hours on Saturdays and Sundays.

41

As he grew, Cesar became increasingly aware of how difficult field work was on his parents. They regularly left home at five in the morning and didn't return for fourteen hours. Most jobs required stooping. Often when his parents returned home at night, they could do little more than fall into bed exhausted. Yet for all of their hard work, their wages were meager. At times the price of transportation to and from a job was nearly as much as they earned all day. Worse still, some growers cheated farm workers out of the tiny wages they did earn. Cesar regularly witnessed field supervisors "miscounting" how much produce a worker harvested or how many hours a person worked. There were growers who insisted workers buy their groceries at company stores which charged inflated prices and gave a share of their profits back to the growers. Another trick was to not pay workers on time and hope they would move elsewhere while waiting for their wages. Cesar's family once worked several weeks without being paid at all.

Such treatment robbed people of their self-respect. One field worker explained:

> We can't afford to lose our jobs . . . so we keep quiet and don't complain and the farmers think we are happy. In the fields the bosses shout at us in front of our wives and families. They insult our

Cesar graduated from eighth grade in 1942 and immediately became his family's primary wage earner.

womenfolk and bully our children. And because we are so poor, we cannot afford to lose the job. We take it. This destroys the family. And it destroys the men as individuals.[4]

Being cheated out of a living wage was not so much an issue of money, Chavez said, but a principle. "It's a matter of destroying your manhood," Chavez said, "taking away all your dignity."[5]

When Cesar's father suffered a chest injury in an automobile accident in 1942, Cesar dropped out of school entirely. He had only completed eighth grade, and though he planned to go back someday, he never had the chance.[6] Instead, Cesar gradually took over his father's responsibilities. He began driving the car and deciding where and when the family would work. Each day in the fields he set a goal and refused to leave until he reached it. One day he told his mother, "From now on, Mother, you're not going to step one foot out of the house to work anymore!"[7] Mrs. Chavez never returned to farm work.

As he grew, the migrant camps and fields that filled these years blurred in Cesar's memory. Various shacks on various farms were his homes, and his days were spent in the field. The family worked year round, traveling from California's Imperial Valley in the south to Sacramento in the north. For the Chavez family, the calendar was divided into crops rather than seasons. During the winter, they worked cabbage and lettuce. In the spring, they tended watermelon and cantaloupe. Summer brought lima beans, corn, and chili peppers. With fall came grapes and cotton. And then the cycle would begin again.

Yet in many respects, Cesar was a typical teenager. He enjoyed being with friends, and he rejected adults' ideas as silly and old-fashioned. He rebelled against his mother's home remedies and quit listening to Mexican music. Instead, he liked the big band music so popular with young people of his time. He and his friends went to dances and dressed distinctively. Their clothing copied a style worn by Mexican-American youth known as *pachucos*. Pachucos wore ducktail hair cuts, pegged pants, long suit coats, and thick-soled shoes. Though some pachucos were blamed for barrio riots, Cesar and his friends simply dressed this way to be fashionable. Cesar was not a troublemaker. Still, his clothing made police suspect him of being up to no good, and at times he was harassed by them.

Cesar's pachuco days ended in 1944. To avoid being drafted into the Army during World War II, Cesar enlisted in the Navy. For the next two years, he worked as a deck hand on the boats used to transport troops. Sometimes he stayed on land,

and he never fought in combat. But Cesar's Navy experience was unpleasant. The ocean made him seasick and a little bit frightened. Worst of all was the discrimination he faced. The most distasteful jobs were given to minorities and few were ever advanced in rank.

Once, while on a six-day pass, Cesar decided to take action against racism. While visiting Delano, California, he went to see a movie at the town's segregated theater. Being Mexican-American, he was supposed to sit in the section reserved for Mexicans, African Americans, and Filipinos. But on that particular day, Cesar was tired of such treatment. He felt like sitting wherever he wanted, just like most of the other people there. So he did. He chose the white side of the theater, and he refused to move. The manager called the police who came and took Cesar to jail. But because Cesar hadn't broken any laws, the police couldn't charge him with anything. Instead, he was given a lecture and let go. Cesar was angry, but satisfied that he had stood up for his rights.[8]

Even after this distasteful incident, Cesar returned to Delano regularly because of a special young lady. Helen Fabela had grown up in the area and attended Delano High School. The two had first met in a malt shop there. While Cesar

Chavez in his Navy days with his friends. Chavez is the sailor on the far left.

was in the Navy, he and Helen dated whenever he could get to Delano. When Cesar was discharged, he returned to the area, and he and Helen continued to date.

Upon discharge, Cesar also returned to the migrant labor he knew so well. During this time, he became increasingly aware of how farm laborers might improve their own circumstances. The Chavez family had always spoken out against injustice, and Librado had taught Cesar that his own dignity was worth more than money. If anyone in the family felt a grower was treating someone unfairly, they would all leave the field, taking as many people with them as possible. Cesar once called the Chavezes "one of the strikingest families in California."[9] But until a day in 1948, Cesar had never experienced a group walkout.

That day Cesar was picking cotton with his family near Wasco when a caravan of cars drove by the field. The passengers were waving flags and shouting *"Huelga! Huelga!"* ("strike") at the workers. These striking farm laborers were urging others to join their protest of low wages. The Chavezes wasted no time in leaving the field and drove off behind the strikers. The group wound its way through the San Joaquin Valley encouraging others to strike. Although the walkout was effective at first, most workers went back to the fields in a few days and nothing changed. The experience, however, left a mark on Cesar. It taught him that a successful strike must involve large numbers of employees who pledge to stick together. Although he didn't know much about labor unions, he had begun to understand the basic concepts which made them successful.

Cesar's father had belonged to unions, and now Cesar began reading everything he could about them. He was especially intrigued by union leaders, and the thought of organizing farm workers began gnawing on the edges of Cesar's consciousness. It would still be a while, though, before these ideas were shaped into a well-defined plan.

At the moment, Helen Fabela occupied most of Cesar's thoughts. The two were married in 1948. On their honeymoon they toured the old Spanish missions that were scattered throughout southern California. Then they settled down to earn a living and raise a family. They first lived in a one-room shack in a Delano migrant camp. They had no electricity or running water there, and their front yard was a quagmire of mud. A small kerosene camping stove struggled to keep the tiny home warm.

Miserable, the Chavezes left and traveled north, first to San Jose, then to join Cesar's parents in a sharecropping venture on a strawberry farm. The Chavezes tended their crop every day for over two years, never making much for their efforts. When it became clear that they couldn't earn a decent living raising strawberries, they packed up and returned to San Jose. There Cesar found work picking string beans for a dollar an hour. But the work was sporadic, and when he heard of jobs four hundred miles north in Crescent City, the Chavezes moved there for a year.

By 1952, Cesar and Helen were back in San Jose, living in Sal Si Puedes across the street from Richard and his family. Cesar took a job at a lumber mill to support his growing family which now included three children. Though he didn't know it then, this last move started Cesar down a path that would lead him into the history books of the nation.

CHAPTER FOUR

THE TRAINING GROUND

 Two people whom Chavez met when he returned to Sal Si Puedes had a profound impact on his life. The first was a Catholic priest, Father Donald McDonnell, who regularly came to the neighborhood to say mass. Because there were no churches in the barrio, services were held in an old hall that Chavez helped clean and paint. McDonnell was about the same age as Chavez, and it wasn't long before the two were friends.

During their time together, Chavez and McDonnell talked about farm workers and their plight. McDonnell understood how large landowners stayed rich by keeping migrant workers in poverty. He showed Chavez photographs of a worker's shack and a grower's mansion, and of a migrant camp and a grower's large office building. From these pictures Chavez came to realize the unjust difference between laborers' wages and growers' profits.

McDonnell also gave Chavez books about outstanding men who were dedicated to helping others. One was about St. Francis of Assisi, a man who lived during the Middle Ages. St. Francis was born to a rich merchant, but he rejected his wealth and devoted his life to the poor. He was a gentle man who preached peace and respect for all living things. The humility and self-sacrifice of St. Francis moved Chavez and reminded him of his mother's kindnesses to the poor.

In addition, McDonnell told Chavez about Mohandas Karamchand Gandhi (1869-1948). Gandhi had made international headlines leading India to independence from British rule. Gandhi's methods were peaceful, but hard-hitting and potent. Most notably, he used fasting, group action, and economic warfare to battle his opponents. Yet Gandhi never compromised his commitment to nonviolence in achieving a goal. Chavez was quick to grasp Gandhi's message of attaining social justice through peaceful means. Perhaps this was because Chavez's mother had already laid a firm foundation regarding the virtues of nonviolence. Chavez would eventually use some of Gandhi's tactics himself.

The second person from Sal Si Puedes who would greatly influence Chavez was Fred Ross. Ross had been hired by a man from Chicago named Saul Alinsky. Alinsky wanted to improve the conditions of poor people in America. He sent Ross to Los Angeles to organize the hundreds of Mexican Americans living there. Ross would create a group called the Community Service Organization, or CSO. The CSO's purpose was to unite people and give them political power. After six years, Ross had firmly established a CSO in Los Angeles. By 1952, he was ready to branch out.

Ross moved to San Jose, another city where many Mexican Americans lived. One of the first people he met there was Father McDonnell. McDonnell immediately told Ross he should talk with Chavez. McDonnell had introduced Chavez to men dedicated to service and nonviolence. Fred Ross took Chavez's education a step further. He showed him how to use service and nonviolence to change people's lives. Of Ross, Chavez said simply, "He changed my life."[1]

In the beginning, however, Chavez had no interest in meeting Ross. Forewarned that Ross was coming to talk to him, Chavez was annoyed. He had spoken with sociologists before who asked personal questions but took no action, and Chavez figured Ross was just another one coming to pry. So on the day Ross was due to arrive, Chavez walked across the street to his brother's. When Ross came, Helen told him Chavez was gone. But Ross was persistent. He came back three more times, and the last time Helen refused to lie. Instead, she pointed to Richard's.

Still, Chavez meant to have the last word. After Ross persuaded him to hold a small meeting in his home, Chavez made plans to sabotage the gathering. He invited the roughest men he knew and served them beer. Before Ross arrived, Chavez instructed the men to listen to Ross politely—until Chavez passed his cigarette from one hand to the other. On this signal, the men were to disrupt the meeting and cause Ross as much trouble as possible. But when the meeting started, Chavez was struck by how much Ross knew about Sal Si Puedes. And a lot of what he said made sense. Ross showed Chavez that the problems of the poor didn't need to be solved one person at a time. Issues could be attacked on a group basis. The other men watched for Chavez's signal, but it never came. Growing impatient, a few began to harass Ross. Chavez promptly told them to leave, scrapping his original plan.

Ross was just as impressed with Chavez at this first meeting as Chavez was with him. He saw immediately that Chavez understood how the downtrodden could acquire power. Ross saw, too, that Chavez had the drive to help others gain this power. Ross once said that the people who would change society would be people "who just cannot live with themselves and see injustice in front of them. They must go after it whenever they see it, no matter how much time it takes and no matter how many sleepless nights of worry."[2] Before Ross went to bed the night he met Chavez, he wrote in his diary, "I think I've found the guy I'm looking for."[3]

Now, after a day's work at the lumber mill, Chavez hurried off to other house meetings with Ross, gatherings much like the one Chavez had held in his home. At the meetings Chavez was quiet, but he watched and listened carefully to everything that went on. Once he was back home, he thought about the things Ross had said and the way the organizer was molding individuals into a cohesive unit. One of the CSO's main goals was getting people registered to vote. Soon Chavez and others were involved in a voter registration drive in Sal Si Puedes. Day after day, they walked through Sal Si Puedes knocking on doors. They talked with the residents about the residents' personal problems and problems common to the poor. Then they told the people how they could affect change by voting for leaders who would help. Little by little, they convinced people to register to vote. Though the others were sporadic in their efforts to recruit voters, Chavez worked each day. For eighty-five nights in a row he traipsed the streets of San Jose, encouraging the people to register. His persistence paid off. By the 1952 general election, the CSO had registered four thousand new voters.[4]

But on election day, disaster struck. When Mexican Americans showed up at the polls to vote, officials asked them if they were American citizens. Some were told to read. Because few were literate and almost all were fearful of authorities, many left the polling place without voting. The CSO was outraged by this harassment. Each person who had been registered was an American citizen with a right to vote. At an emergency meeting, the CSO leaders wrote a letter of protest to the United States attorney general. Because the leaders were afraid of losing their jobs, none would sign the letter—until Chavez stepped forward. Doing so won him respect and recognition throughout the community.

Soon Chavez was spending more and more

time working with the CSO. To build a power base the Mexican Americans needed voters. To vote one had to be a United States citizen. Though many Mexicans qualified for citizenship, they had never become official citizens. So Chavez helped them with the necessary paperwork and coached them for their citizenship tests. One thing led to another, and before long Chavez was representing people at places like the welfare department, the doctor's office, and the local school. Gradually, Chavez learned to ask the people he assisted to help the CSO. Of this exchange, Chavez once said, "I was willing to work day and night and go to hell and back for people—provided they also did something for the CSO in return."[5]

When Chavez was laid off at the lumber mill Ross convinced Alinsky to hire him as a CSO organizer. Chavez's first solo assignment was to create a CSO chapter in DeCoto (now Union City), California. Chavez had watched Ross long enough to understand how to proceed. Still, he was nervous. Basically a shy person, Chavez was also small. At five foot six inches he looked young and wasn't sure people would listen to him. When he arrived at his first house meeting, he was too frightened to go inside. Instead, he drove up and down the street trying to build up the courage to go in. When he finally entered the home, he found a seat in the corner and stayed quiet until he was forced to identify himself as the leader of the meeting. But Chavez needn't have worried. His soft, dark eyes and handsome native features inspired confidence. In a short time, he was leading house meetings throughout DeCoto, and a new CSO was born.

Next, Chavez went to Oakland. Again he organized house meetings that drew only a handful of people. Yet in the small groups, people felt comfortable speaking about what was on their minds. Still not an accomplished public speaker, the people may have been more comfortable than Chavez. Though shy, Chavez was obviously sincere when explaining how the CSO could help solve problems. After several successful house meetings, Chavez invited the small groups to a large meeting. After a few large meetings, the organization was ready to elect local officials. At this point, Chavez's work was done, and he moved on to start again somewhere else.

Small successes bolstered Chavez's confidence, and he was ever watchful to learn more about organizing. He traveled from one town to another creating CSO chapters—Madera, Bakersfield, Hanford. Chavez never stayed in one place longer than four months. People liked his easygoing manner and boyish grin. They felt comfortable with Chavez—he drove an old car, dressed in work clothes, and had been a migrant worker himself. Most of the people with whom Chavez spoke were field workers, and they quickly realized he understood the pain they suffered from spending hours in the field.

Of the many injustices growers imposed on their laborers, Chavez found the short-handled hoe the most demeaning. He believed that growers were inhumane for requiring people to work doubled over all day long swinging a hoe only eighteen inches long. Chavez said the growers must see their employees as tools to show such little consideration for the torture they endured. Of the growers' use of the short-handled hoe, Chavez said, "There is no need for such cruelty. I never want to see that again, not until I can do something about it."[6]

But Chavez was patient. "When you organize," he once said, "you must do it bit by bit, very deliberately and carefully. It's like digging a ditch. You take one shovelful at a time."[7] Chavez didn't mind spending hours with a worker to make sure he understood how the CSO could be of benefit.

As he traveled through the small towns of California, Chavez was getting better and better at organizing people. He learned early how important it was to involve people in creating change for

Chavez found working for the CSO rewarding. In this 1950s photo he poses (second from the right) with other CSO organizers.

themselves. "We are not helpless," he would tell those gathered at the small house meetings. "We are not pawns. If we get together, and stick together, we can change things. We can make a difference."[8] Chavez, in his quiet but charismatic way, made people feel their own power. Later, many would describe a "presence" Chavez carried that inspired those around him. Some even said he had a spiritual aura. Author Richard A. Garcia called this quality a kind of "humble innocence that is the bearer of the words of another world."[9]

Chavez was also a good listener. When he went to Oxnard in 1958 (the same place he had spent a miserable winter as a child), he planned to get a CSO started and begin registering voters. But when he listened to the people at various house meetings, he quickly realized they weren't interested in voting. Their immediate problem was the *braceros*. A bracero is a citizen of Mexico who has permission from the United States government to work as a farm laborer in the United States. Many growers bussed braceros across the border to work in their fields because they worked for less money and in worse conditions than the American migrant laborers. Therefore, growers could increase their profits if they used braceros instead of Americans. But United States law said that braceros could only be used when there were not enough Americans to tend the fields. Unfortunately, some of the growers around Oxnard were ignoring this law and in so doing were putting many local farm workers out of work.

For thirteen months Chavez fought against the growers' use of braceros. He protested and filed complaints with local, state, and federal authorities. He organized demonstrations and staged a sit-in at one ranch. But his most effective ploy was a march he directed through Oxnard. Chavez estimated that ten thousand people joined the march which was filmed by several television stations. All of the attention sparked an investigation that finally forced the growers to stop hiring braceros. It was 1959 and Chavez had just orchestrated his first major victory for farm laborers. He was thrilled!

As growers began using the Oxnard CSO office as a hiring hall for farm workers, Chavez reflected on what he had learned. The struggle had not been without sacrifice. During the long year, Chavez had worked daily from five in the morning until ten at night. He had lost twenty-five pounds. But this mattered little to Chavez. He had organized hundreds of people with nonviolent tactics and achieved his goals. He had shown workers how their field labor could be converted into power against the growers.

As a CSO organizer, Chavez headed up a voter registration drive in Oxnard. This 1959 campaign was successful largely due to the commitment of volunteers such as these.

The Oxnard experience convinced Chavez that it was time to begin what he had been thinking about doing for many years. It was time to build a union of farm workers. Chavez knew that others had tried before but had failed. Wealthy farmers had been using poor people to keep themselves rich for decades. During that time, they had become experts at squelching periodic protests.

With the help of other growers and local authorities, anyone who had tried to organize farm laborers had been threatened, jailed, and even beaten. On more than one occasion, people had been killed fighting for better working conditions.

The people with whom Chavez shared his dream were also aware of the many failures of previous organizing attempts. Almost everyone disapproved of his plan to create a farm workers' union. Only Helen believed it could be done. Though she was quiet, she was behind her husband all of the way. Helen's own family had a history of fighting for social justice. When she had lived in Mexico, her grandfather had fought with the Mexican revolutionary, Pancho Villa.

Helen later said she had never doubted that Chavez would succeed in building a union. Perhaps this was because she knew of the intensity of his desire. Or maybe it was because she knew how persuasive her husband could be.

Unfortunately, each time Chavez brought up the idea of forming a farm workers' union to the CSO it rejected his proposal. Instead, the CSO leadership convinced Chavez to become its national director in Los Angeles. With eight children and a $150 per week salary, it was an offer Chavez at first couldn't refuse. But two and one-half years later, Chavez knew this wasn't what he wanted

By 1961, Chavez had organized people in several California towns. Yet his work had just begun. This map shows many of the places of importance in Chavez's life.

to do. Again and again, he tried to talk the CSO's leadership into letting him organize a farm workers' union. Over and over, they said no. By 1962, Chavez had made up his mind. He felt he had no other choice when he announced to CSO directors, "If CSO doesn't go for this farm labor project, I'm going to leave the organization."[10] It didn't. He did.

With $1,200 in the bank, the Chavezes moved to Delano to begin the task of creating a union for migrant workers. In Delano, they reasoned, Helen's family could help them if times got rough. Although he didn't know if he would succeed, Chavez knew he had to try. And the thought terrified him.

HUELGA!

One reason Chavez chose Delano as the place to build a union was because Helen's family lived nearby. Another reason was that the thirty-eight thousand acres of grape vineyards around Delano needed tending all year round. This meant farm workers lived in the area and didn't have to move from one crop harvest to another. Chavez felt a union would have the best chance of succeeding in an area with a stable labor force.

Chavez began his organizing by drawing a map of all the farm workers' camps in the San Joaquin Valley. There were eighty-six. Then he drove through the valley observing the camps, farms, crops, and workers. Occasionally, he stopped and asked field workers how they felt about a union. Most of their responses weren't encouraging. This didn't stop Chavez.

Quietly, so as not to arouse the attention of the growers, Chavez began organizing. Using the same methods he had perfected in the CSO, Chavez first arranged small house meetings. During these meetings, he asked workers what they thought would be a fair wage. He also asked about their other problems and told them he was organizing an association to help them. Chavez continued to visit farm fields, too.

In the meantime, Helen worked in the fields. At first, Chavez was frightened. He wondered how he would feed his family and pay his bills. "But by the time I had missed the fourth paycheck and found things were still going, that the moon was still there and the sky and the flowers, I began to laugh," he later said. "I really began to feel free."[1]

Chavez often took his youngest child, three-year-old Anthony, with him while he canvassed the area. Chavez also recruited other family members to get the union started. After school on Fridays, he took his children with him to nearby towns to hand out leaflets about the union. There were now eight Chavez youngsters—Fernando, Sylvia, Linda,

Elouise, Anna, Elizabeth, Paul, and Anthony. Chavez would drive into the neighborhoods where farm workers lived and divide the leaflets amongst the youngsters. As the children ran up and down the streets passing out the information, other neighborhood children joined them. Soon, the area was covered, and the family moved on to another town.

Manuel Chavez, Chavez's cousin, also became a part of the organizing effort. At the time, Manuel was earning over one thousand dollars a month selling cars. When Chavez asked him to help, Manuel wanted to know how much he'd be paid. Chavez told him nothing. Manuel promptly told Chavez he was crazy! But Chavez wouldn't take no for an answer. The cousins had grown up and worked the farm fields together. Chavez reminded Manuel of this and of his obligation to help others. Finally, Manuel agreed to help for six months. He would stay for many years.

It took Chavez longer to recruit his brother, Richard, but he eventually did. He enlisted others, too. The Reverend Jim Drake was an early organizer for the union. Chavez's commitment infected Drake who was passionate about ending the exploitation of farm workers. Drake would remain an important figure in the union for several years. Another early convert was Dolores Huerta, a woman Chavez knew from his CSO days. Huerta was a mother of three who gave up her job with the CSO to help start the union.

The Chavez garage became the union's headquarters, though Chavez was not often there. Much of the time he was out in the fields or at someone else's home. Just as he had done in his CSO days, Chavez helped solve whatever problem a person had. And all of the time he helped, he talked about the union. Before long, Chavez was known for his kindness, and workers were coming to him for aid. In this way, Chavez established rapport and trust with the people he wanted to organize. But as Jim Drake observed, "The pains taken by Cesar were never part of an act. They were a very real extension of his philosophy that human beings are subjects to be taken seriously."[2] One by one, Chavez and his organizing crew convinced laborers to join the union. According to Drake, "That's how [Chavez's] union was built: on plain hard work and these very personal relationships. It was a slow, careful, plodding thing."[3]

By the fall of 1962, enough farm workers had joined the union to hold a convention. Fresno was chosen as the site, and a meeting was scheduled in an abandoned theater. On September 30, 1962, when the first convention of the National Farm

Workers Association (NFWA) came to order, about two hundred people were in attendance.

Behind the podium hung a huge flag Manuel had created, a flag Chavez hoped would become a symbol of unity to the members. Chavez and Manuel had considered the flag's design carefully. They wanted a bold, easy-to-recognize flag that

Dolores Huerta, Antonio Orendain, and Cesar Chavez at the NFWA's first convention in 1962. Behind them is the flag designed by Manuel Chavez.

striking workers could duplicate by hand. Temporarily covered with paper, Chavez waited until the right moment to dramatically unveil it. When he did, the audience's response was less than enthusiastic. Many members, in fact, didn't like anything about the black Aztec eagle in a circle of white surrounded by a red background.

Quickly, Chavez explained the symbolic nature of the flag. Red and black flags were traditionally used by striking workers in Mexico, and the eagle was a sacred bird of the Aztecs, the people from whom many farm workers descended. The eagle was also the national symbol of Mexico and the United States. Manuel defended the flag, too. He described the black as the dark situation of the workers, the white as hope, and the red as the struggle and sacrifice needed to build a union. Then he added, "When that damn eagle flies, the problems of the farm workers will be solved!"[4]

With this comment, the flag was adopted by the members. A Union motto was also adopted that day, *"Viva la causa!"* which means "Long live the cause!" Later the farm labor movement was often referred to as *"La Causa,"* meaning "the fight for justice."

The conventioneers set NFWA dues at $3.50 a month. This was a lot of money for farm workers. They would have to make sacrifices to pay their monthly dues. But Manuel argued that if the workers wanted a union, they would have to sacrifice for it, just as the leaders were doing. At the convention, two hundred farm workers became dues-paying members. After ten months, all but twelve had dropped out.

Chavez, however, would not give in to disappointment. When he began his crusade, he had pledged to work hard for three years before giving up. He had also vowed to create an independent union, one which could operate in whatever manner the members desired. This meant the Union could not become a part of another established union. Nor could Chavez accept money from sources which might have strings attached. Already he had turned down offers of financial assistance in order to maintain the Union's independence. He also declined a $21,000-a-year job offer for himself. Instead, he chose to work as the NFWA leader for five dollars a week. But Chavez didn't consider himself especially righteous. He demanded the same personal commitment and internal strength from everyone who joined the NFWA.

In 1963, recruitment efforts started all over again. Working eighteen hours a day, Chavez, Manuel, Huerta, Drake, and a few others continued their work. Of Chavez, Huerta once said, "Cesar Chavez is both a strong leader and a taskmaster. He demands production. He will say, don't tell me what you plan to do. Tell me what you've done."[5] Always looking for ways to get to the people, the NFWA sometimes threw a fiesta or barbecue for workers so they could sign up members. During these early years, Chavez found that once a person had paid dues for six months, he or she would become a solid union member who would never leave.

While Chavez built his fledgling union, the rest of America struggled with race relations. African Americans all over the country were tired of discrimination and poverty. Some advocated violence, and race riots erupted in several cities across the nation. Others, such as Dr. Martin Luther King, Jr., opposed violence. King's followers staged peaceful demonstrations and protests against racial hatred and unfair laws.

But African Americans weren't the only ones fighting discrimination. The Civil Rights Movement of the 1960s involved people of many races. Mexican Americans, as well as other minorities, were active in the struggle for social equality. Many white Americans joined in the fight, too. One of the most powerful of these was President John F. Kennedy. He urged the United States Congress to pass laws which would prohibit race discrimination and segregation. When Kennedy was assassinated in 1963, many minority citizens felt they had lost a true friend. Still, the Civil Rights Movement continued to grow.

And so did the NFWA. One thousand farm workers had joined the Union by August of 1964.[6] Although the membership was large, Chavez knew the NFWA was still in its infancy. It would be a long time, he felt, before the Union would be ready for a strike. Unfortunately, the NFWA was not given that time.

In the summer of 1965, another small association of farm workers walked off their jobs in the vineyards around Delano. Though Chavez didn't want to strike yet, he didn't have much choice. It was a universal pact between unions that one union would not work where another union was striking. Therefore, if the NFWA wanted the status of a real union, it had to support others who were striking.

Chavez called a membership meeting for September 16th. The date held special significance for the Mexican people. It was Mexico's Independence Day. At the meeting, Chavez reminded members of the ten-year-long struggle Mexicans had once fought to free themselves from Spanish rule. Then he said, "We are engaged in another struggle for the freedom and dignity which poverty denies us. . . . Tonight we must decide if we are to join our fellow workers in this great labor struggle."[7] Other speeches followed, speeches frequently interrupted by shouts of "Viva la causa!" When excitement in the hall was at its peak, a vote was taken and the NFWA membership decided to go on strike.

There was much to do. Several times, Chavez asked growers to meet with the Union. None would. So Chavez called meetings to discuss NFWA strategy. Again and again, workers were warned not to use violence. Chavez felt that violence would only bring on more violence. Although the growers were wealthier than the NFWA, the workers were not without leverage. There were powerful nonviolent tactics the Union could use. Chavez emphasized that how the NFWA struggled was just as important as winning the battle.

On the first day of the strike, twelve hundred farm workers refused to work. This emptied about four hundred square miles of vineyards around Delano. But the growers soon hired nonunion employees to work the fields. These people were known as "strikebreakers" because if enough of them worked, the strike would fail, or be "broken."

According to their instructions, Union members formed picket lines along the roads that bordered the fields. Carrying signs bearing the NFWA flag or the word huelga, the workers walked back and

When the NFWA called its first strike in 1965, hundreds of workers picketed fields carrying signs like this one.

forth shouting to the strikebreakers. They called out their complaints against the growers and urged those working to stop and join La Causa.

The growers were angry. Some reacted violently, and one even pointed a shotgun at strikers and threatened to kill them. Other growers walked amongst the picketers, elbowing them or knocking them to the ground. Some growers drove trucks and tractors along the edges of the fields and covered the strikers with dust. But in the face of this harassment, the NFWA members remained nonviolent.

When television and newspaper reporters interviewed the growers, they maintained that farm workers were happy with their wages and working conditions. They claimed that Chavez had little support amongst the majority of the workers. They even accused him of being a Communist.

The local police seemed to believe the growers. They kept watch over the NFWA office, followed Union members, and photographed strikers, writing reports on each. The police also decided that strikers should not shout at the workers in the field. The NFWA felt this was an infringement of their right to free speech. In a calculated move, Chavez asked for volunteers to challenge this policy. Repeatedly, he made it clear that any volunteer might be arrested. With instructions to walk the picket line just as before and shout at strikebreakers even if the police told them not to, the volunteers left for the fields. It wouldn't be long before they were arrested.

Chavez had planned this challenge for the day he was to speak at the University of California in Berkeley. After learning that the arrests had been made, Chavez went in front of the students and explained the farm workers' situation. Then he told them about the forty-four strikers who had just been arrested for shouting. Chavez asked the students to skip their lunches and instead donate the money to La Causa. Chavez took this same message to three other colleges that day. He went back to Delano with $6,700.

Soon Chavez was recruiting help from people other than farm workers. Some of the earliest and best volunteers were those who had been active in the Civil Rights Movement in the South. Chavez was especially happy to have these people because many were trained in nonviolent protest. Other volunteers were students, some were from church organizations, and still others were ordinary, everyday people. Chavez liked the cross-section of people working with the NFWA. He believed that people with different backgrounds brought new ideas to the Union and kept it growing intellectually.

To the diverse Union supporters, Chavez was a great leader. He was firm and unwavering and willing to wait a lifetime to reach his goals. His eyes were at once sad and soft, and he was forever brushing back a shock of dark hair. On occasion, Chavez was still the mischievous child who liked to play tricks. Even when things looked gloomiest, Chavez was capable of humor. But he was also capable of great anger. Sometimes he pounded his fist on a table to make a point and his voice could become stubborn and hard. Yet underneath the anger was a steady calm, an undeniable commitment that moved others to action.

Once the strike was under way, the NFWA began a new tactic—the boycott. During a boycott, the general public is encouraged to stop buying a particular product in support of a cause. If enough people participate, a boycotted company can't make money. This often forces the company to negotiate with whomever has called the boycott. At the beginning of the NFWA boycott, members followed truckloads of grapes as they rolled out of Delano. As the trucks reached their destinations, the workers climbed out of their cars and formed picket lines wherever the grapes were being delivered. In December, the NFWA decided to narrow its boycott to only one grower. Chavez carefully chose Schenley Industries which owned about 3,350 acres of grapes near Delano. These grapes represented only one of several Schenley products. Chavez reasoned that by boycotting all of the Schenley merchandise, the company could quickly be hurt financially. If so, Schenley should then be happy to settle the strike with the grape workers to preserve its other products.

Chavez chose thirteen major cities across the United States to become boycott centers. He sent volunteers to these cities who recruited about ten thousand more people to picket stores and encourage the public to boycott Schenley. As farm workers and volunteers walked picket lines throughout the United States, the movement gained national attention and support. By March of 1966, the strike had drawn the attention of the U.S. Senate Subcommittee on Migratory Labor. Senate members came to Delano to investigate the strike, among them Senator Robert Kennedy, the brother of the slain president, John F. Kennedy. After seeing the situation for himself, Senator Kennedy became an avid supporter of the farm workers' cause.

Next Chavez employed another nonviolent, but hard-hitting tactic to keep the NFWA fight in the national spotlight. He organized a 250-mile march from Delano to Sacramento, California's capital city. There, farm workers would present their case to Governor Edmund Brown. The walk would take twenty-five days, and the marchers planned to arrive on Easter Sunday.

Sixty-seven Union members began their walk in Delano. The leader carried an American flag. Behind him marchers carried the flag of Mexico, the NFWA flag, and huelga signs. Some held a banner of Our Lady of Guadalupe, the patron saint of Mexico. Our Lady of Guadalupe was revered by the Mexican Americans and Catholics in the Union. But the NFWA was diverse. Not everyone was of Mexican heritage, nor was everyone Catholic. There were many white, African-American, Asian, Jewish, Protestant, and even agnostic members. Many of these people didn't like having La Causa so closely associated with a Catholic saint.

But Our Lady of Guadalupe was a powerful image. She was native in appearance and represented the poor. Many Mexicans believed she had first appeared to a Mexican peasant in 1531. Since that time she was thought to be a protector of the downtrodden and had been worshiped for centuries. Peasant armies carried banners of her in the Mexican Revolution and Our Lady had become a national as well as religious symbol. It only seemed natural, then, that many would want to carry her image in the NFWA march. For them, the march itself was as much a sacred act as a political act. The deep faith of the Catholics in the Union could not be suppressed. Against the wishes of some, the march proceeded with the banner of Our Lady of Guadalupe.

At the end of the first day, Chavez had a swollen ankle and a huge blister. Yet he refused to take painkillers or rest. By the second day's end, Chavez's right leg was swollen to the knee. Still, he would not stop. After one week of marching, though, Chavez became so ill he had to be driven behind the marchers.

As the farm workers passed through the small towns along the way, the local people greeted them with enthusiasm and held rallies for the workers. At the rallies, copies of the Schenley boycott pledge were distributed. They read, "I will not buy Schenley products for the duration of the Delano farm workers' strike. Get with it, Schenley, and negotiate. Recognize the National Farm Workers Association."[8]

Support and press coverage for the NFWA increased at each stop. The mayor of Fresno held a luncheon for the marchers. In Modesto, the Union was met with a show of support from other unions, and in Stockton five thousand people came out to voice their support. Stockton was important for another reason. Here Chavez

For much of the 1966 march to Sacramento, California, Chavez needed a cane to help him walk. Marchers followed Chavez carrying a banner of Our Lady of Guadalupe.

received a phone call from Schenley saying the company was finally ready to negotiate an agreement with the NFWA.

In the middle of the night, Chavez traveled back to Los Angeles to talk. Schenley signed an agreement recognizing the NFWA as the laborers' representative. In addition, the company agreed to use the Union hall for hiring workers and to give their field laborers a thirty-five cent an hour raise.

It was raining on Easter when the marchers entered Sacramento. Governor Brown had left town, but ten thousand other people greeted the marchers. Chavez was there, too. As a cheering crowd gathered at the steps of California's capitol building, words which had been written before the march began were read. "Our Pilgrimage is the match that will light our cause for all farm workers to see what is happening here, that they may do as we have done. . . . History is on our side. May the Strike go on. *Viva La Huelga! Viva La Causa!*"[9]

The Schenley breakthrough was a great victory. But the work had just begun.

BOYCOTTS, A FAST, AND VICTORY

 Schenley was only one of several growers, and the NFWA now needed to convince others to sign contracts. Less than one week after the Sacramento march, the NFWA began picketing DiGiorgio, a large corporation which owned vineyards around Delano and in other regions of California. Some of DiGiorgio's field workers were already NFWA members, but they felt they could not afford to stop working. Chavez understood this and he used them as informants to keep the Union aware of what was happening on the inside.

In May, DiGiorgio obtained a court order that allowed only a few strikers at a time to picket its fields. This crippled the Union. Without large numbers of people walking the picket lines, the strike lost its effectiveness. The farm workers were frustrated. Chavez called a meeting and told the people he had no ideas about what to do next. But, he added, he had faith that together they would come up with a nonviolent solution. He was right. Three women asked if the court order prohibited them from praying at DiGiorgio's fields. This idea was the gem Chavez was looking for. He promptly told Richard to build a chapel on the back of his station wagon. Once finished, Chavez parked his car across from DiGiorgio's gates, complete with a shrine of Our Lady of Guadalupe.

Next, the NFWA spread leaflets around the area inviting farm workers to an evening mass at the DiGiorgio ranch. Hundreds of people came. For the following two months, mass was held daily at the station-wagon chapel. Before long, workers from DiGiorgio's fields were attending the services, too. After each mass, the NFWA signed up new members. Chavez believed the prayers were instrumental in raising people's spirits, and he called the vigil "a beautiful demonstration of the power of nonviolence."[1]

In the meantime, DiGiorgio invited the Teamsters'

Union into its fields to recruit members. Chavez adamantly opposed the Teamsters. In 1957, a United States Senate investigation found that Teamster officials had illegally spent union funds for personal possessions. In addition, the investigation revealed that the Union had links with organized crime. Not only did Chavez feel the Union was corrupt, but he also believed that the Teamsters intimidated people into joining its ranks. Furthermore, Chavez knew that the Teamsters made contracts with companies without first consulting the union members. These contracts, Chavez felt, benefited the company, not the workers.

Though the Teamsters were allowed into DiGiorgio's fields, the NFWA was not granted the same privilege. When the farm workers' union protested to Governor Brown, he appointed an arbitrator to handle the situation. The NFWA asked for two things. First, it wanted the same opportunity to talk to DiGiorgio workers as the Teamsters enjoyed. Second, the NFWA wanted a secret ballot election to find out which union the workers wanted to represent them. The arbitrator granted both requests. A few days later, DiGiorgio laid off 190 NFWA members.[2]

Still, Chavez was hopeful about the upcoming election. At it, workers would be able to decide which union—the NFWA, the Teamsters, or the AWOC (a small union associated with the national AFL-CIO union)—would represent them. Chavez knew this election's outcome was vital to the NFWA. If it lost, the Union would be finished. Believing his Union was fighting for its life, Chavez launched a crusade that left little to chance. NFWA members were tightly organized to campaign amongst the DiGiorgio workers. Daily meetings taught recruiters how to present information and handle opposition from Teamsters. Chavez went a step further.

The NFWA and AWOC had talked about merging before, and Chavez felt they must do so now. Together, the two unions had a better chance of beating the Teamsters. But merging meant the NFWA would lose its independence, and not everyone liked this. However, Chavez was firm. He told the members, "We've got to think about the future of the Union. . . . We need strength. We need allies."[3] Most members agreed. In August of 1966, the NFWA and the AWOC officially became one union affiliated with the AFL-CIO. In time this new union, the United Farm Workers Organizing Committee, would become known as the UFW. Balloting at DiGiorgio began at 6:00 A.M. on August 30. At 8:00 P.M. the voting box was locked into the trunk of a California highway patrol car and driven to San Francisco. The votes were counted the next day. Back in Delano, Union members waited anxiously for the results. The announcement came at 10:30 that morning: UFW—530; Teamsters—331.[4] Chavez had led the UFW to another major victory, and the people were elated!

In addition to farm workers' support, the UFW was beginning to feel encouragement from the rest of America. Soon after winning the DiGiorgio election, Chavez received a telegram from Dr. Martin Luther King, Jr. It read, "The fight for equality must be fought on many fronts—in the urban slums, in the sweat shops of the factories and fields. Our separate struggles are really one—a struggle for freedom, for dignity, and for humanity."[5]

In the summer of 1967, the UFW felt strong enough to strike the largest table grape grower in the region, Giumarra. When Giumarra obtained an injunction to keep a minimum number of strikers around their fields, the Union shifted its thrust. Chavez sent fifty volunteers to New York City to organize a boycott. As 1968 began, Giumarra countered by placing several different labels on its grape boxes to confuse consumers. With up to sixty separate labels, it became impossible for the Union or consumers to keep track of which grapes were Giumarra's. The boycott stalled. Then Ross

The first UFW grape boycott encouraged people all across America to stop buying grapes. This Sacramento supermarket is being picketed by supporters.

and Huerta came up with a solution. They proposed extending the boycott to all grapes. Chavez opposed this plan, not wanting to penalize uninvolved growers. But because Giumarra was using other growers' labels on its boxes, Huerta reasoned they must be in on the plan. Therefore, she said, they too should be held accountable. As they had many times before, Huerta and Chavez argued. Of their disagreements, Huerta said:

> The people working under Cesar were over-whelmed by him. . . . They [won't] fight with him. When I think he's wrong, or when I think my way is better, I fight with him. . . . We've had some bloody fights . . . he is stubborn.[6]

This time, Huerta won. Although reluctant, Chavez called for a nationwide boycott of all California-grown table grapes. Union members were sent out to Boston, Chicago, Los Angeles, and Detroit. By contacting local labor unions, churches, students, and civic groups, the boycott gained momentum. Newly recruited volunteers picketed supermarkets asking shoppers not to buy grapes. From this boycott came a secondary boycott—a call for consumers to completely avoid shopping at stores which carried California grapes. The boycott spread, and the public rallied to the cause.

While the Union was receiving more publicity than ever, Chavez tried to remain in the back-ground. He did not want to be an irreplaceable leader, and he winced at being put into the public spotlight. When Union members had buttons made with his picture on them, he became angry. The Union was La Causa, not Cesar Chavez.

Gradually, though, Chavez came to accept being the symbol of the Union. He knew it was a burden he must bear if the UFW was to succeed. The important thing was working to see La Causa's goals realized.

The grape boycott seemed to be a successful step. Chavez later called the boycott a nearly perfect nonviolent struggle. Nonviolence, Chavez said, required mass involvement as well as action, and the grape boycott produced both. Thousands of consumers could participate in it easily, showing both strength and power through peaceful actions—all they had to do was stop buying grapes and quit shopping at certain stores.

Though grape growers began losing money, they still refused to negotiate with the UFW. The longer the strike lasted, the more frustrated the workers felt. Some wondered if their children would have to finish the strike for them. When people talked of resorting to violence, Chavez felt he must reassert his nonviolent stance. At a Union meeting he talked for an hour about the need to maintain peaceful resistance. He told the workers that violence would destroy all that the Union had worked for. Then he announced that he was going on a fast to renew his commitment to nonviolence and La Causa. He ended his speech by saying, "I am doing this because of my love for you."[7]

Chavez's fast affected people in different ways. While growers accused him of performing a publicity stunt, civil rights leaders voiced their support. Many of the Mexican Americans in the UFW understood the fast as a religious act. Personal penance was a deep tradition in their culture, and they believed Chavez was sincere in his sacrifice of food for the good of the Union. But some people worried that UFW work would be halted during the fast. Others were concerned for Chavez's health. A small segment of the Union criticized Chavez, saying he was "playing Jesus Christ."[8]

Chavez ignored the negative comments and moved a bed into his UFW office. He knew that without food he would become weak, and he was determined to work as much as possible. Chavez kept a straw crucifix and a small image of Our Lady of Guadalupe in his office. The walls were decorated with photographs of Gandhi, Martin Luther King, Jr., and Robert Kennedy. According to one observer, "The spirit of martyrs fills the room."[9]

Even the forty acres of land the office sat on was special. The Union had acquired the plot in 1966, and Chavez had plans for the site. Appropriately named Forty Acres, he hoped it would one day become a center for migrant farm workers. He wanted the land to house Union offices, medical clinics, legal aid services, and even

94

During Chavez's 1968 fast, UFW members and supporters prayed at Forty Acres every night.

classrooms. In Chavez's dream, the various buildings would be made of adobe with red tile roofs. And, like the old Franciscan missions he loved so much, a high adobe wall would surround them all. Inside the wall a central plaza with gardens and fountains would provide a peaceful place for UFW members to relax. For now, though, there was no time to build the center at Forty Acres. Other, more pressing matters commanded the Union's attention.

On the first night of Chavez's fast, friends pitched a tent at Forty Acres to express their support. The second night more tents appeared, along with a priest who said mass. Each night after that, mass was held and the number of tents increased. Farm workers came from all over to pray for Chavez and the Union. Many brought offerings—some religious, others symbolic. The fast, along with the prayer vigils and outpouring of devotion had a profound effect on Chavez. He felt freed from the day-to-day details of running the Union, and he was able to focus more clearly on the larger picture. After serious reflection, he knew his purpose in life was to fight for social justice.

But more than a personal act of worship, the fast was beneficial to the entire Union. As it continued, Chavez saw Union members pull together and work harder. Public sympathy for La

Causa increased, too. Messages from a myriad of people expressed concern and admiration for Chavez and the UFW. Although unintentional, Chavez's fast made him the voice of America's poor and drew more public attention to La Causa.

By the twenty-first day of Chavez's fast, his doctor insisted he take some medication and a small amount of nourishment. As more days passed, workers and family members pressured Chavez to end his fast. Finally, after twenty-five days Chavez felt ready to eat again. He had lost thirty-five pounds and was terribly weak. Bundled against the March cold, he was carried to an outdoor mass in a Delano park. Senator Kennedy had come to be a part of the occasion and he served Chavez the communion bread which broke his fast. Later Kennedy spoke, calling Chavez "one of the heroic figures of our time."[10]

By 1969, growers claimed they were willing to negotiate with the UFW. But the contract they offered was little better than what the workers already had. Still, some Union members argued, it was a contract. Union recognition was the breakthrough, not the specific terms of the agreement. They believed that once any contract was signed, its terms could be strengthened each time it was renewed.

When Chavez disagreed, he angered many.

When Chavez broke his first fast, U.S. Senator Robert Kennedy was present. Seated next to Kennedy is Chavez's wife, Helen.

Top AFL-CIO officials were annoyed, church support wavered, and calls poured into the UFW office. Though under tremendous pressure, Chavez would not be moved. He felt the growers and the Union were just too far apart to settle. He was not going to rush into a contract simply because it was now profitable for the growers to do so. The workers had waited four years to sign an agreement. Chavez wondered if the growers had suddenly forgotten about those long years "of badgering us . . . putting people out of a job, and bringing in strikebreakers."[11]

Chavez knew the boycott was hurting the growers financially. One opinion poll found that seventeen million Americans were boycotting grapes. It was reported that over six million boxes of grapes were stockpiled in various warehouses. Stores in major cities had stopped carrying California grapes, and TWA airlines refused to serve them. The boycott had even stopped grapes from being unloaded at docks in England, Sweden, Norway, and Finland.

In 1970, growers finally decided to give in to Union demands. Catholic bishops with experience in labor relations offered their help in working out a contract. After several meetings, the bishops brought the two sides to agreement. On July 29, 1970, Union members packed the meeting hall at Forty Acres to watch growers finalize the historic agreements. Twenty-six contracts were signed that day. Each one included substantial gains for farm workers.[12]

Afterward, Chavez spoke. "The strikers and the people involved in the struggle sacrificed a lot," he said. "Ninety-five percent of the strikers lost their homes and their cars. But I think that in losing their worldly possessions in order to serve the poor, they found themselves."[13]

Chavez had sacrificed a lot, too. During the past five years, his determination and faith had been continually tested. Not only had he been fighting the growers, but he had also been settling skirmishes inside the UFW. For some, La Causa became a symbol of Mexican-American heritage and Chavez a Mexican-American folk hero. These people resented persons from other backgrounds participating in the Union. But from the outset, Chavez had made it clear that the UFW belonged to all farm workers. "Why be racist?" he had asked. "Our belief is to help everyone, not just one race. Humanity is our belief."[14] Furthermore, Chavez refused discussion regarding this matter. "On discrimination," he said, "I don't even give the members the privilege of a vote, and I'm not ashamed of it."[15]

Chavez had also sacrificed his home life for the UFW. He could be gone for weeks at a time, and when he was in town, his children were often asleep before he came home. One night, as Chavez lay in bed, he looked up to see his son's name written on the ceiling. Chavez knew this was the boy's way of saying he should pay more attention to him. While speaking of his relationship with another son, Chavez lamented, "I never once took him fishing or to a ball game or even to the movies."[16]

Furthermore, Chavez had sacrificed his own well-being to La Causa. The fast had weakened his body and aggravated a back problem that periodically sent him to bed for days at a time. He had been locked in jail for the good of the cause. He had gone for years without a vacation. But even on the most stressful of days, Chavez never lost sight of the people for whom he was fighting. Huerta once said of him, "I've never seen Cesar harsh with a worker. . . . He is a very gentle guy—a very gentle guy in many ways."[17]

Having succeeded in California's vineyards, the UFW planned to go after contracts from the California lettuce growers. But when the UFW won the grape contracts, the lettuce growers raced to sign agreements with the Teamsters. Chavez was infuriated. He knew this had been done to keep the UFW out of the lettuce fields. Prepared for another long battle, the Union asked for elections to let the field workers determine which union they desired. When elections were denied, the UFW held strikes and boycotts. For the next several years, the Union would be locked in one battle after another with the Teamsters.

By 1973, public support for the UFW had decreased. President Nixon's administration seemed to favor the Teamsters and the growers. The strong public support the Union had enjoyed during the grape boycott had faded. In addition, the tragic assassinations of Dr. Martin Luther King, Jr., and Senator Robert Kennedy had left the UFW without two of its most powerful allies. Sensing weakness, the grape growers saw their chance to destroy the UFW once and for all. Instead of renewing the UFW contracts they had signed in 1970, they signed contracts with the Teamsters.

Though its troubles had now multiplied with the loss of the vineyard contracts, the UFW refused to die. Chavez continued the fight which often turned ugly with violence instigated by the Teamsters. Union members were beaten, shot at, and their property destroyed. Some were even killed. Bomb threats were called into the Union office. Sometimes Teamsters were arrested for their acts of violence, but more often brutalities went ignored. Chavez himself received death threats serious enough to send him into occasional hiding. At times, Union members insisted he be accompanied by bodyguards. In spite of the violence directed at the Union, Chavez was constantly reminding members of their commitment to nonviolence. He severely reprimanded anyone who defied this order.

In 1974, Chavez was invited to meet with Pope Paul VI in Rome. At the meeting, the Pope praised Chavez's work and told him his methods could help poor people all over the world. Also in 1974, Edmund (Jerry) Brown, Jr., was elected governor of California. The new governor was sympathetic to La Causa, and he actively campaigned to help farm workers. He was instrumental in getting the California legislature to pass the Agriculture Labor Relations Act in 1975. This law required growers to recognize an elected union.

Chavez was ecstatic about the passage of the law. With renewed vigor, he led one clash after another to rid California's fields of the Teamsters. Behind him were fiercely loyal men and women who shared his dream that someday farm workers all across America would enjoy their fair share of the nation's bounty.

THERE IS MORE TIME THAN LIFE

 By 1977, thousands of farm workers were represented by either the UFW or the Teamsters. Though both unions had managed to win better and better contracts, they were still battling one another. Suddenly, the Teamsters asked for a truce. Tired of fighting, Chavez eagerly agreed. In March, the two leaders signed a pact which allowed the Teamsters to organize farm cannery workers and truck drivers. The UFW would have exclusive rights to the workers in the fields. The agreement applied to thirteen western

states and the UFW looked forward to increasing its organizing efforts outside of California.

The Union had already been recruiting workers in Arizona, Texas, and Florida. The majority of the nation's migrant laborers, however, were still not represented by any union. The UFW had only scratched the surface of the hundreds of thousands who lived in America's South and who annually traveled throughout the Midwest and the East. Most of these migrants were African-American, and they faced the same horrible working and living conditions as the workers in the West. Largely through the UFW organizing efforts, farm laborers in states outside of California were called to the nation's attention and began gaining a political voice.

When the UFW-Teamster peace pact expired in the early 1980s, the Teamsters again began re-cruiting field workers. This time, though, the Teamsters didn't use violence and intimidation. Now they worked cooperatively with the field la-borers. Throughout the 1980s, Teamster numbers grew while UFW membership declined. By the early 1990s, about twenty thousand people be-longed to the UFW, a dramatic decrease from its 1972 peak of nearly one hundred thousand.[1]

There were many theories as to the cause of the UFW's decline. Growers and workers alike blamed Chavez's leadership, charging that the Union's sloppy record keeping, untrained negotiating teams, and inconvenient hiring procedures drove people away. In part, these problems were caused by Chavez's reliance on a staff of volunteers who worked six long days each week for nothing more than room, board, and a low wage. This reflected Chavez's belief that Union workers must dedicate themselves totally to La Causa. He had once said, "If we're going to lead people and ask them to starve and to really sacrifice, we've got to do it first, do it more than anybody else, because it isn't the orders, it isn't the pronouncements, it's the deeds that count."[2] Chavez himself earned only $5,000 per year, the average annual income of a farm worker.

But the austere living conditions exhausted volunteers, and they seldom stayed longer than two years. When inexperienced ones took their places, the new volunteers needed training, a process that stole time from other Union tasks. In addition, the mistakes they inevitably made were harmful to the Union. Realizing this, some members questioned Chavez's dependence on volunteers. They wanted the UFW to hire well-educated staff people who specialized in various aspects of union management. A reasonable salary would encourage the specialists to stay with the

Union for several years. But Chavez continually rejected proposals to do this.

A few insiders suggested that these refusals pointed to a deeper problem with Chavez's leadership. Though the UFW had needed his strong guidance in its beginning, some believed he was now too accustomed to having total control of the Union. As the UFW grew and its areas of operation spread, Chavez rarely delegated responsibilities. Several talented and dedicated Union workers were allowed to do nothing more than follow orders. And just as the Union had once blossomed from a cross-section of people and ideas, it wilted under oppression.

Furthermore, local UFW officials were not elected by the farm workers, but appointed by the Union's executive board. Therefore, the opinions and concerns of the field laborers were not always represented when Union decisions were made. This was a far cry from the days when Chavez talked with many Union members personally, learning about each one's individual needs. Some people traced the beginning of Chavez's detachment to 1977 when he moved the UFW head-quarters out of Forty Acres. That year, Union offices were relocated on donated land in the mountains near Keene, California. Chavez named the new site La Paz, which means, "The Peaceful

Place." UFW business was then handled by officials and volunteers who lived at La Paz. Chavez and Helen lived there, too.

Moving the UFW headquarters away from the farm fields removed Chavez from the close physical contact he had always had with the field workers. As time passed, many laborers became discouraged by what they perceived as the Union's inattention to them. Several either joined the Teamsters or simply dropped their UFW membership. Others tried to work within the UFW to bring back local representation and control. But Chavez strongly opposed them, and even fired longtime Union workers who disagreed with his position.[3] To many laborers, it seemed that the Union no longer belonged to the workers, but to Chavez himself. According to one, "too many workers felt used and deserted; and opposition to the UFW grew."[4]

Yet Chavez defended his actions by saying that his interests went beyond the issues of salaries and benefits. He wanted to improve the lives of poor people in many ways. In so doing, he experimented with yoga, personal encounter programs, holistic medicine, and meditation. Some people felt this desire to build a social movement rather than a labor union was a handicap to the Union. A few proposed that Chavez give up control of the

Union if his goal was achieving social justice rather than fair pay for field laborers. Chavez, however, maintained that the UFW could do both.

In addition to its internal struggles, the UFW faced trouble from external sources. In 1983, it lost a valuable friend when Democratic Governor Jerry Brown was replaced by Republican George Deukmejian. Agribusiness had spent one million dollars helping Deukmejian get elected, and once he was governor, he continually supported the growers' side of farm issues. Many thought Governor Deukmejian's leadership contributed significantly to the UFW decline.

Another external factor affecting UFW memberhip was the increasing number of illegal immigrants who poured into the United States daily to work in the farm fields. Few wanted to risk angering their employers with demands for better pay or working conditions. But rough waters didn't deter Chavez. Dolores Huerta reported, "He is at work at five-thirty or six o'clock in the morning; everybody else comes in at eight o'clock. He works on into the evening. He works Saturdays and Sundays."[5] Chavez had seen this kind of perseverance pay off in the past. During the last two decades, the real wages of California farm workers had increased by 70 percent, and many migrants now had access to pension plans, disability insurance, health care benefits, credit unions, and the right to bargain. Many observers called these achievements a minor miracle. The Union's current setbacks were not going to keep Chavez from finishing the job he had begun.

Migrant farm workers were still America's most unprotected, underpaid workers. Astonishingly, a 1980s study found that more than one third of the country's farm workers still did not have access to toilet facilities in the fields, and one half were not provided with drinking water.[6] Yet in 1985, the United States Occupational Safety and Health Administration still refused to require growers to provide toilets and water.[7] The UFW continued to fight for these basic necessities.

Chavez also stepped up his campaign against the use of pesticides, an issue the Union had been addressing for many years. As far back as 1969, physicians and public health officials had warned growers that farm workers were being poisoned by the chemicals used in the fields. Toxic pesticides gave laborers skin rashes, eye irritation, nausea, and respiratory problems. Worst of all, hundreds of farm workers died each year from exposure to pesticides.[8] In 1987, Chavez initiated another grape boycott that asked consumers to avoid grapes that had been sprayed with one or more of five pesticides the United States Environmental

Protection Agency had deemed harmful. In 1988, Chavez embarked on a fast for this cause that would last thirty-six days.

But working tirelessly for La Causa finally took its toll. Chavez's Union trip to San Luis, Arizona, in 1993 would be his last journey. There, on April 23, the sixty-six year old died in his sleep. He was less than fifty miles from the place of his birth. Chavez left behind his wife, eight children, twenty-seven grandchildren, one great-grandchild, three brothers, and two sisters.

News of Chavez's death traveled fast and affected people deeply. California state flags were lowered to half-mast, and condolences poured in from around the world. A final march for Chavez was planned, a march to honor the man who had changed so many lives. For this last walk, Chavez was dressed in the fancy embroidered shirt he wore on special occasions, and he was laid in a plain pine coffin Richard had made. On April 28, crowds gathered at Forty Acres to keep vigil through the night. By morning, thirty-five thousand people had come to Delano. Many were celebrities and government officials, but there were also thousands of farm workers, some who had traveled long distances to be there. Hundreds had brought their children. One migrant worker, with tears in his eyes, lifted his grandson high to see

In 1988, Chavez fasted for thirty-six days to protest the use of pesticides in farm fields. Jesse Jackson and Ethel Kennedy (wife of the slain senator Robert Kennedy) came to California to express their support.

Chavez's face and told the child, "See this man. I am going to tell you about him someday."[9]

Carrying red and black banners and Union flags, the mourners followed Chavez's casket out of Delano to Forty Acres. Along with Chavez's several friends and family, the Reverend Jesse Jackson and three of Robert Kennedy's sons took turns as pallbearers. At the end of the march, Cardinal Roger M. Mahony conducted mass. The cardinal, dressed in a Mexican *serape* (shawl), read a message from Pope John Paul II. Then Chavez's grandchildren placed a short-handled hoe and a wooden UFW eagle on the altar. When the memorial ended with a performance by Mexican-American musicians, the group's leader told Chavez good-bye. "Cesar, we have come to plant your heart like a seed. You shall never die. The seed of your heart will keep on singing, keep on flowering, for the cause."[10]

Indeed, La Causa is alive. Four of Chavez's eight children live at La Paz today and work for the Union. Arturo Rodriguez, Chavez's son-in-law, is the current UFW president. As such, he continues to strive toward Chavez's vision of union representation for all field laborers.

It is estimated that there are as many as five million migrant farm workers in the United States today. Predominantly African-American and Hispanic

Today, thousands of children still live in poverty while their parents follow the sun to harvest America's bounty.

people, they still wend their way north through the farm fields each year. These gatherers of the nation's food have a disability rate five times greater than any other American worker. They suffer from a host of illnesses ranging from noise-induced hearing loss to tuberculosis. Pesticide exposure sickens three hundred thousand of them each year. Yet in spite of these dangers, many earn salaries lower than the minimum wage. They have no paid holidays, sick days, overtime, retirement, or disability benefits. Some must still go into fields with their children. And tragically, most migrant youth never make it through the ninth grade.

However, many field workers have not lost hope. They believe they can make a better tomorrow. This, perhaps, is Cesar Chavez's greatest legacy. His creation of a union from a handful of ordinary farm workers proved his unfailing belief in what he called "the genius of the people."[11] Across the country, leaders of small unions fashioned in the same style as the UFW, work toward improving the migrant's life. Fernando Cuevas, one of Florida's two hundred thousand migrant laborers, is one such leader. Cuevas is second-in-command of the Farm Labor Organizing Committee, a union that has won contracts for thousands of field workers. And another union leader, Carlos Marentos, organizes farm laborers for the Border Agricultural Workers Union in New Mexico and Texas. Many migrant labor leaders learned about the power of group action from Cesar Chavez. In their own way, they continue his work.

The creation of these unions, coupled with the UFW's work, pay tribute to Chavez. From his example, union leaders understand that their mission requires dedication and patience. Chavez, himself, knew the fight would take time. Throughout his lifelong struggle for justice, he often repeated a favorite dicho—*"hay más tiempo que vida"* ("there is more time than life").

But Chavez had accomplished much in his life. Many believe he did more for migrant farm workers than anyone else in America's history. In 1994, his family and friends established the Cesar E. Chavez Foundation to keep his spirit alive. Also in 1994, Chavez was posthumously presented with the highest civilian honor a United States citizen can receive, the Presidential Medal of Freedom. The medal was accepted by Helen in Chavez's name as well as in the name of all people who work for justice.

In Chavez's fight for justice, he became a folk hero for millions of Mexican-American people as well as for poor people everywhere. Along his

After Chavez's death, he was awarded the Presidential Medal of Freedom. Here President Clinton, with Hillary Clinton beside him, presents the award to Helen Chavez. Arturo Rodriguez, the current president of the UFW, is standing next to Helen.

journey, Chavez's path was strewn with obstacles most people would have found insurmountable. Yet as America watched and marveled, Chavez accepted these challenges, meeting each one, a step at a time. During his life, he encountered human nature at its best and at its ugliest. At times he felt frustrated, downhearted, confused, and angry. Yet Chavez never deviated from his commitment to nonviolence and peaceful protest. At the end of his 1968 fast, Chavez said:

> When we are really honest with ourselves, we must admit that our lives are all that really belong to us. So it is how we use our lives that determines what kind of men we are. It is my deepest belief that only by giving our lives do we find life.
>
> I am convinced that the truest act of courage, the strongest act of manliness is to sacrifice ourselves for others in a totally nonviolent struggle for justice. To be a man is to suffer for others. God help us to be men![12]

Truly, Cesar Chavez had been a man.

CHRONOLOGY

1927— Cesario (Cesar) Estrada Chavez is born near Yuma, Arizona.

1937— When delinquent taxes become due on the Chavez farm, the family travels to California for work, hoping to earn enough to pay their tax bill.

1939— The Chavezes' efforts are futile, and their farm is sold at a public auction. The family moves to California permanently to become migrant farm workers. Cesar also works to help his family get by.

1942— Chavez graduates from the eighth grade and begins field work full time.

1944— Chavez joins the Navy to fight in World War II.

1948— Chavez marries Helen Fabela.

1952— After moving to San Jose, Chavez meets Fred Ross, a CSO organizer. Chavez works for the CSO in his free time, then becomes a full-time organizer himself.

1962— Chavez resigns from the CSO to create the NFWA, a union for farm workers.

1965— Led by Chavez, the NFWA begins its first strike and boycott, targeting California grape growers.

1966—The CSO joins the AFL-CIO, which will eventually become known as the UFW.

1968—Chavez embarks on his first fast that lasts twenty-five days and garners nationwide support for farm workers.

1970—When grape growers sign contracts with the UFW, the strike and boycott end. Chavez then calls for a nationwide boycott of lettuce.

1973— Instead of renewing their contracts with the UFW, grape growers sign contracts with the Teamsters. Battles for contracts and membership ensue between the UFW and the Teamsters.

1977— As the UFW and the Teamsters negotiate a truce, Chavez pledges to rebuild his decimated union.

1988—Chavez embarks on a thirty-six-day fast to protest the use of pesticides in farm fields.

1993— Chavez dies in Arizona on April 23.

1994—The Cesar E. Chavez Foundation is founded, and Chavez is posthumously presented with the Presidential Medal of Freedom.

Chapter Notes

CHAPTER 1

1. Jacques E. Levy, *Cesar Chavez: Autobiography of La Causa* (New York: W.W. Norton and Company, 1975), p. 74.

2. Robert Lindsey, "Cesar Chavez, 66, Organizer of Union For Migrants, Dies," *The New York Times* (April 24, 1993), p. 29.

3. Sandra Weiner, *Small Hands, Big Hands* (New York: Pantheon Books, 1970), p. 29.

4. Peter Matthiessen, *Sal Si Puedes* (New York: Random House, 1969), p. 77.

5. Ibid.

6. Weiner, p. 37.

7. Matthiessen, p. 253.

8. Jan Young, *The Migrant Workers and Cesar Chavez* (New York: Julian Messner, 1972), p. 75.

9. Ibid.

10. Richard Mines, Susan Gabbard, and Beatriz Boccalandro, *Findings From the Agricultural Workers Survey (NAWS) 1990* (San Mateo, Calif.: Office of Program Economics, 1991), p. 26.

11. Young, p. 69.

12. Weiner, Introduction.

13. Ibid.

CHAPTER 2

1. "Papers, 1951–1971 (Predominantly 1962–1971)," The United Farm Workers, Office of the

President Collection, Walter P. Reuther Library, Wayne State University, p. 1.

2. Jacques E. Levy, *Cesar Chavez: Autobiography of La Causa* (New York: W.W. Norton and Company, 1975), p. 24.

3. Ibid.

4. Ibid. p. 21.

5. Consuelo Rodriguez, *Cesar Chavez* (New York: Chelsea House Publishers, 1991), p. 25.

6. Levy, p. 40.

7. Rodriguez, p. 26.

8. Levy, p. 40.

CHAPTER 3

1. Ronald B. Taylor, *Chavez and the Farm Workers* (Boston: Beacon Press, 1975), p. 64.

2. Peter Matthiessen, *Sal Si Puedes* (New York: Random House, 1969), p. 224.

3. Ibid.

4. Leonard Greenwood, "Farm Labor Trouble: Some Still Seek Peaceful Solution," *Los Angeles Times* (November 17, 1968), pp. G:1, 2.

5. Jacques E. Levy, *Cesar Chavez: Autobiography of La Causa* (New York: W.W. Norton and Company, 1975), p. 61.

6. "Papers, 1951–1971 (Predominantly, 1962–1971)," The United Farm Workers Office of the President Collection, Walter P. Reuther Library, Wayne State University, p. 1.

7. Levy, p. 72.

8. Consuelo Rodriguez, *Cesar Chavez* (New York: Chelsea House Publishers, 1991), p. 32.

9. Levy, p. 78.

CHAPTER 4

1. Consuelo Rodriguez, *Cesar Chavez* (New York: Chelsea House Publishers, 1991), p. 37.

2. Jacques E. Levy, *Cesar Chavez: Autobiography of La Causa* (New York: W.W. Norton and Company, 1975), p. 95.

3. Rodriguez, p. 39.

4. Jan Young, *The Migrant Workers and Cesar Chavez* (New York: Julian Messner, 1972), p. 86.

5. Levy, p. 111.

6. Ronald B. Taylor, *Chavez and the Farm Workers* (Boston: Beacon Press, 1975), p. 64.

7. Mark Day, *Forty Acres* (New York: Praeger Publishers, 1971), p. 114.

8. Joan London and Henry Anderson, *So Shall Ye Reap* (New York: Thomas Y. Crowell Company, 1970), p. 181.

9. Richard A. Garcia, "Cesar Chavez: A Personal and Historical Testimony," *Pacific Historical Review* (May 1994), p. 227.

10. Levy, p. 146.

CHAPTER 5

1. Consuelo Rodriguez, *Cesar Chavez* (New York: Chelsea House Publishers, 1991), p. 48.

2. Jacques E. Levy, *Cesar Chavez: Autobiography of La Causa* (New York: W.W. Norton and Company, 1975), p. 163.

3. Peter Matthiessen, *Sal Si Puedes* (New York: Random House, 1969), p. 58.

4. Levy, p. 175.

5. Dolores Huerta, "Reflections on the UFW Experience," *Center Magazine* (July/August 1985), p. 7.

6. Matthiessen, p. 60.

7. Levy, p. 184.

8. Rodriguez, p. 67.

9. Jan Young, *The Migrant Workers and Cesar Chavez* (New York: Julian Messner, 1972), p. 125.

CHAPTER 6

1. Consuelo Rodriguez, *Cesar Chavez* (New York: Chelsea House Publishers, 1991), p. 75.

2. Jacques E. Levy, *Cesar Chavez: Autobiography of La Causa* (New York: W.W. Norton and Company, 1975), p. 235.

3. Ibid. p. 240.

4. Joan London and Henry Anderson, *So Shall Ye Reap* (New York: Thomas Y. Crowell Company, 1970), p. 158.

5. Levy, p. 246.

6. Ronald B. Taylor, *Chavez and the Farm Workers* (Boston: Beacon Press, 1975), p. 186.

7. Jan Young, *The Migrant Workers and Cesar Chavez* (New York: Julian Messner, 1972), p. 148.

8. Levy, p. 274.

9. Ibid. p. 293.

10. Robert Lindsey, "Cesar Chavez, 66, Organizer of Union For Migrants, Dies," *The New York Times* (April 24, 1993), p. 1.

11. Rodriguez, p. 79.

12. Ronald B. Taylor, "Huelga! The Boycott That Worked," *The Nation* (September 7, 1970), p. 168.

13. Mark Day, *Forty Acres* (New York: Praeger Publishers, 1971), p. 167.

14. Richard A. Garcia, "Cesar Chavez: A Personal and Historical Testimony," *Pacific Historical Review* (May 1994), p. 231.

15. Matthiessen, p. 143.

16. Ibid. p. 291.

17. Levy, p. 265.

CHAPTER 7

1. Leonel Martinez and Hugo Martinez-McNaught, "Young, Old Come to Delano to Say Farewell," *Bakersfield Californian* (April 30, 1993). A-1.

2. Jacques E. Levy, *Cesar Chavez: Autobiography of La Causa* (New York: W.W. Norton and Company, 1975), p. 242.

3. Evan T. Barr, "Sour Grapes," *The New Republic* (November 25, 1985), p. 23.

4. Frank Bardacke, "Cesar's Ghost," *The Nation* (July 26/August 2, 1993), p. 132.

5. Dolores Huerta, "Reflections on the UFW Experience," *Center Magazine* (July/August 1985), p. 8.

6. Henry Weinstein, "The Health Threat In the Fields," *The Nation* (May 11, 1985), p. 558.

7. Ibid.

8. Ronald L. Goldfarb, *A Caste of Despair* (Ames, Iowa: The Iowa State University Press, 1981), p. 35.

9. Patt Morrison and Mark Arax, "For the Final Time, They March for Chavez," *Los Angeles Times* (April 30, 1993), pp. A:1, 28–30.

10. Ibid.

11. Richard A. Garcia, "Cesar Chavez: A Personal and Historical Testimony," *Pacific Historical Review* (May 1994), p. 225.

12. Levy, p. 286.

FURTHER READING

Holmes, Burnham. *Cesar Chavez*. Chatham, N.J.: Raintree Steck-Vaughn, 1992.

Levy, Jacques E. *Cesar Chavez: Autobiography of La Causa*. New York: W.W. Norton and Company, 1975.

Matthiessen, Peter. *Sal Di Puedes*. New York: Random House, 1969.

Rodriguez, Consuelo. *Cesar Chavez*. New York: Chelsea House Publishers, 1991.

Ross, Fred. *Conquering Goliath: Cesar Chavez at the Beginning*. Detroit: Wayne State University Press, 1992.

Weiner, Sandra. *Small Hands, Big Hands*. New York: Pantheon Books, 1970.

INDEX